Dishing With the Kitchen Virgin

Dishing With the Kitchen Virgin

SUSAN REINHARDT

KENSINGTON BOOKS
http://www.kensingtonbooks.com

KENSINGTON BOOKS are published by

Kensington Publishing Corp.
850 Third Avenue
New York, NY 10022

All Kensington titles, imprints and distributed lines are available at special quantity discounts for bulk purchases for sales promotion, premiums, fund-raising, educational or institutional use.

Special book excerpts or customized printings can also be created to fit specific needs. For details, write or phone the office of the Kensington Special Sales Manager: Kensington Publishing Corp., 850 Third Avenue, New York, NY 10022. Attn. Special Sales Department. Phone: 1-800-221-2647.

Kensington and the K logo Reg. U.S. Pat. & TM Off.

ISBN-13: 978-0-7582-1709-7
ISBN-10: 0-7582-1709-9

First Kensington Trade Paperback Printing: May 2008
10 9 8 7 6 5 4 3 2 1

Printed in the United States of America

For my family, without whom I'd have no love. Or material.

Acknowledgments

I'd like to thank my mother for trying to teach me how to cook. She gave it her best effort, though I successfully resisted. I'd also like to thank everyone who was a part of this collection, either with their stories, diets, recipes or humor. Without my friends and family, and readers of my columns, the book wouldn't have been possible.

Big thank-yous go to my wonderful and superprofessional agent, Ethan Ellenberg, and the talented and tireless staff at Kensington including those who design the great covers, the sales team and my excellent editor, Audrey LaFehr, who, like Ethan, believed I could write funny.

I appreciate my children, Niles and Lindsey, for enduring a mother whose face for the past couple of years has been plastered against a computer screen. Without their patience and understanding, I'd be another would-be writer who had no time to place words on the page.

Finally, and as always, praise for the Read It Or Not, Here We Come Book Club members, especially Laurie Pappas, who founded the group and who actually reads EVERY selection. Her grace is limitless.

One last thing, I'm grateful to the *Asheville Citizen-Times* for helping promote the books once they're published. This includes Polly McDaniel (my editor), Tony Kiss (entertainment editor), and John Boyle (columnist), who've all done stories about the books.

Oh, and Webman Randy. If you need a great website, he's the ticket.

Contents

FOREWORD

Dishing With the Kitchen Virgin

Thirty years ago I decided to honor my parents' anniversary with a partially home-baked cake, choosing Duncan Hines's yellow mix for the base unit, topped with what I imagined to be made-from-scratch fudge frosting, worthy of my long-married, oft-suffering parents.

The suffering parts were due to the misbehaviors of their two teenaged daughters, me and Sister Sandy, two years younger, who Mama says made her hair turn gray and gave her two blue bags beneath her eyes.

Nothing like Crisco and sugar icing to make up for coming home tipsy one night and passing out as Mama lectured on the dangers of drinking and how it could lead to an assortment of societal ills, including and foremost, unwanted pregnancy and life in a series of low-income rentals and trailer parks.

Guilt is why I didn't buy the icing already prepared, even though common sense would tell a 15-year-old kitchen virgin she has no business baking or topping anything whipped up from scratch.

I spent most of an entire morning working on this debut cake, and the house smelled like a bakery in high gear, giving off that warm, fuzzy, everything-is-wonderful-in-life feeling.

All was going beautifully until I scanned the recipe and found it called for three egg whites.

"Egg whites?" I turned toward my 13-year-old sister who followed me like a little puppy into every situation but trouble.

"The shell part, moron," she said and stuck out her giant front teeth the dentist kept promising her face would grow into. "Anybody could figure that one out."

This didn't seem right. "I don't think you're supposed to stick the shells in with the sugar and Crisco, are you? I've never had a cake with eggshells in it."

"Well, what other part is white? I told you to buy the canned icing. You have no idea what you're doing."

I did some thinking. If I hard-boiled the eggs, then I'd have a more edible egg white. And so such was the route we took, followed by deyoking and chopping the whites into the icing mixture. We were dismayed to see marshmallow-like lumps poking through the chocolate icing as we frosted the cake, and in the end, we trashed the eggy abomination and bought a Sara Lee.

Thirty years have passed and not much has changed in my kitchen. Often I find myself sitting at the rectangular oak table, once again choking on my own cooking, perhaps holding a Ragú-splattered recipe in hand and wondering, "Where did I go wrong?" Why is it the recipe never turns out for me, even though I read the directions to a tee?"

These rare forays into the kitchen typically occur when I tire of the cafeteria life and that prison-guard barking of one forced to choose a meat way too fast for the brain to register. It is on those occasions I produce my little-used BI-LO Bonus Card, go shopping and prepare optimistically for a normal meal: a meat and two vegetables. Sounds so simple.

I will, at this time, acknowledge that some women (and men) purely enjoy cooking, and may God love them and reward them in Heaven with top-of-the-line cookware and 24-hour access to the Food Network. The rest of us want to get on with our lives and are looking for the easiest ways out while still remaining alive and fairly healthy.

We'd rather not spend two hours a day over our ranges and sinks, unless someone special is coming for dinner and I've yet to meet anyone *that special*. I will, however, watch and enjoy the sassy cooking shows and vicariously produce major feasts courtesy of Emeril and Rachael Ray. I also love reading recipes in cookbooks and magazines, dreaming of the day I might actually concoct something that resembles the photographs of those delectable dishes.

This is as far as it usually goes unless a carcass that will fit in my Crock-Pot is on sale at BI-LO. That's not really even cooking since all you have to do is Stop, Drop and Roll it in salt and pepper, maybe add some chicken broth or Lipton Onion Soup Mix and voilà! The family's happier than a preacher sneaking Bud Lites during a Dinner on the Grounds.

The good thing is, with Crock-Pots, you can throw in raw and even unwashed, unpeeled vegetables and they come out tasting pretty good. If some potato grit ends up in someone's mouth, you can be fairly sure they'll just think they chipped a tooth.

Whoever invented the Crock-Pot gadget deserves the Nobel Peace Prize. Maybe he or she can share it with the Tuna Helper inventor. More on the utter joys of Tuna Helper later.

On a recent night when I attempted a meal from ingredients on hand, my family mostly stared at the barely recognizable platter plop and pushed the dried-up, parched lasagna around on their plates.

An hour later I heard my husband pouring a bowl of Total, and it was then I decided not to cook from recipes again, but to remain loyal to those tried-and-true food companies that never let me down: Banquet, Stouffer's, Campbell's, Pillsbury and Betty Crocker.

I've learned how to take a tacky premade or boxed meal and class it up with cheese and a colorful side dish—one you don't have to cook such as a fan of raw fruits and vegetables. If you can draw a fan shape, you can arrange the carrots and strawberries (or any other fruits and vegetables) in this very fashion.

I've tried many times to evoke homemade smells in the home, going as far as putting a pan of butter and onions on the burner, and letting them sizzle to spread that 5-star-restaurant aroma throughout the house. One can smell a kitchen full of Taco Bell or KFC for only so long.

Plus, the neighbors can see if you're always coming home with take-out and fast-food bags, and they will talk behind your back no matter how Christian and decent you might think they are. In the South, and probably all over the world, being willing and able to cook remains a standard by which some measure decency.

This is one reason it's a good idea to at least perfect a few doable recipes, such as a cake with chocolate icing, minus the hard-boiled egg whites.

It is my belief that anybody can learn to cook, and if not, he or she can at least get by without starving or completely toppling the government's dietary guidelines and food pyramid. We can, with a few simple tricks, fool people into believing we know our way around an oven and four burners and aren't chained and locked to the microwave and Crock-Pot.

I decided to write this book—a wild collection of food-related stories, culinary missteps and dining disasters including recipes at the end of each chapter—for all my fellow cooking virgins, women who, if given a winning lottery ticket, would hire a personal chef first and foremost.

Those things we once wished for—the hot boyfriend who used to be a Hollister model, the old man with a trust fund and weakening pig-valve heart, the tummy tuck for ourselves and personal relationship with a discount plastic surgeon; would march silently behind the desire for magical skills from a personal chef, one who would do all our chopping, dicing, blanching, parching and poaching. He would also shop for the right ingredients and understand how to read recipes or deliver his own scrumptious signature dishes. It goes without saying we'd lose weight and look wonderful due to the combination of his ingredients, our increased heart rates from looking at him and the selections rich in Omega 3 fatty acids he'd fix.

Those of us wanting a personal chef more than anything money could buy wouldn't care how the chef looked as long as he knew how to make our Pyrexes bubble. He could be real ugly. Dog ugly. Ugliest thing alive and weighing 400 pounds with a weenie the size of a miniature golf pencil. It matters not as long as he can wield a spatula, fill our pots and pans, and make mealtimes full of joy, harmony and good health.

While we are dreaming of the day our chef comes in, this is the book for all of us who have felt guilty because our pot holders don't have the burn marks of a real kitchen queen, whose pans aren't scratched and half-scorched from overuse, whose Cuisinart has never been taken from the box and even still sports the old, yellowing bows from the Land of Unwanted & Unopened Wedding Gifts including Salad Shooters and Chop Wizards.

It's for those of us who use our woks as potato chip bowls, who click on the blender only when Bacardi is involved and who believe the person who invented Tuna Helper—particularly the Creamy Parmesan style—should win the Nobel Prize for family harmony.

We are a group of human beings known as kitchen virgins, even though we may dabble and concoct the occasional meal when guilt slaps our conscience and our children say things like, "Chelsea's mother cooks over a stove and says microwaves and fast foods are for lazy sloths and mothers on meth."

"Well, Miss Chelsea," I might (if PMSing) retort, "has a mother who doesn't have three jobs and a husband who won't eat most of her meals. That snuffling hog she wed will gobble anything she throws on the table."

I might be more inclined to cook, too, if my household members didn't groan or complain of stomachaches every time

I attempted a real meal. It might be easier to stand with flour and raw-meat juices running down my forearms if, in the end, someone would say, "Hmmmm, ummm" with every bite and talk about how delicious the food was.

Instead, I hear things like: "Mom, this chicken is so tough I need the electric hedge trimmers to get the gristle out."

"It's pure white meat," I tell them. "No gristle. Best you can buy . . . Butterball."

"My orthodontist said not to eat your meats," my teenaged boy once said. "No offense, Mom."

I don't get it. I used the only gadget besides the microwave I can work, the Crock-Pot, which is designed to make everything tender and edible. Why, I'll bet some people could take an old work boot, pour in some Lipton's Onion Soup Mix and it'd turn out tender as baby greens.

"Sorry, Mom," my son has said more than once. "You're a great mother, but Nana and Mama Peg are a lot better at cooking. Don't feel bad. Everybody has special gifts."

Oh, he's mimicking me. I should have never given him the old "special gifts" speech when he brought home a few clunkers from school or was a benchwarmer for the basketball team.

Now, I *could* cook. Really. If I wanted to. If I put my heart and hands into it. The fact is, they aren't, and the only time I ever enjoyed cooking was when I was soused and doused in wine while everything simmered and burbled on the stove. After three Cabernets, all my meat "Helpers" were French cuisine.

I've noticed that quite a few people who cook and sip booze tend to enjoy the experience. And if their dinner guests drink, too, they will eat just about anything and rant with pink cheeks about how drop-dead delicious everything tastes.

Cooking while intoxicated (CWI) is a condition more common than one may realize, and strikes women and moms, as well as men positioned like soldiers at the grill, flames rising and cooler of beer perspiring in the heat.

This CWI phenomenon is no doubt the reason some people are able to get through the holidays and meal preparations without going into cardiac arrest. Just about every woman I know who loves cooking also imbibes as she coats raw chicken in a Parmesan cheese mixture.

So how does one know if she's a kitchen queen or kitchen virgin or something in between? It goes without saying or testing that if you don't own a single skillet, you are beyond virginal. But if you've tried and still not hit at least half a dozen home runs, then go ahead and wear the crown and sash of one of us Proud Kitchen Virgins.

If one is consistently able to cook from scratch, she is a kitchen hooker, a person who takes a basic recipe and uses tricks of the trade to make it profitable and edible.

Catering doesn't count. That's like saying you've lost your virginity to a sex toy.

From roadkill to redneck spaghetti, from a first-timer's experiences with sushi to a veteran mother's shaving her collard greens with a Daisy double blade, this collection candidly uncovers others' cooking feats and defeats and offers the recipes and stories served upon the buffets of buffoonery.

Bon Appétit!

Or, as I like to say when cutting those cooking corners, "Bon Appe-Cheat!"

Chocolate Scream Cake

Buy a box of Duncan Hines or Betty Crocker yellow cake mix, preferably the kind with the pudding in it for extra moistness.

Follow directions on back of box. To ice the cake: use two cans of chocolate fudge frosting.

The frosting is the secret, the touch that catapults the cake from a "hmmm" to a flat-out scream.

CHAPTER ONE

There Are No Pot Holders in Heaven

My mama used to say she couldn't wait to die, not just because she'd get to meet Jesus and Elvis, in that order, but also because it would finally mean never having to think up another meal.

"I'll be trading my burned pot holders for a pair of smooth white wings," she cooed, the smell of onions frying in butter circling the room like a culinary halo. "I can't wait to close that oven door for good."

Mama would groan and carry on as she flung open cabinets and slammed pots and pans onto the counter in preparation for yet another breakfast, lunch or dinner.

The only time I ever heard her cuss was while cooking or sewing, the latter of which she finally gave up, shoving her Singer in the attic after deciding the effort put forth didn't equal the end result. Since she was a stay-at-home mom, she was expected to carry on with the dinners and meal planning, as this was the sixties and seventies, in a town where the only fast-food restaurant was a Burger Chef until a McDonald's finally came to roost.

Cooking, while she'd never fully admit it, drove Mama near-about crazy, the great effort and imagination of conjuring new ways to present her family of four a pretty-looking supper that didn't drain the life out of her and one that consisted of more than a single color. She hated nights when the colors didn't go right and she ended up with an entirely brown or orange meal.

Brown meals are an aesthetic disaster for anyone and usually consist of baked potatoes, country-fried cube steak, pinto beans and cabbage boiled way beyond the green and into a gummy beige that even the toothless can manage with ease. Lots of people from my part of the South cook green vegetation until it's dog-fur brown.

Topping off one of her brown meals with chocolate ice cream, and Mama would glance at the table and all but cry out, "Why can't I seem to fix a dinner that has more than one color scheme?"

She did the same wailing on nights she made macaroni and cheese and served it with cantaloupe and a salad with Seven Seas French Dressing. She might choose peach sherbet to go along with it all and then once again wonder why she couldn't produce a dinner in multiple hues.

"Everything's orange," she'd say, throwing her glistening hands, coated with the sheen of various food greases, into the air.

My daddy was an excellent sport about it. He knew if he drank enough bourbon after work, anything she made would be edible.

"Two or three highballs or a few Bloody Marys, and I'd moan and sigh with every bite I took," he said. "That's the secret all cooks know. Get 'em sauced before you serve them."

When Mama first got married at the tender age of 19, my Granny, her mother-in-law, nearly fell over dead upon learning Mama didn't know how to make a tossed salad. She learned fast, and we grew up on bland, nearly clear iceberg lettuce served with a couple of slices of cucumber and a tomato wedge covered in a Thousand Island dressing made from swishing together Duke's Mayonnaise and Hunt's Ketchup. If Mama felt creative, she'd toss in some pickle relish.

While her meals were often strange and brown, she did manage to give us a multiple vitamin every day for good measure. She knew she wasn't the best cook or the worst on our street and town, but I know it made her mad every Wednesday when the newspaper hit the curb and she unfolded the page to see the *chosen* woman occupying the most popular and coveted feature, the "Cook of the Week," grinning in all her glory and highfalutin recipes.

This "Cook of the Week" feature came about in the days long before Martha Stewart marched onto the scene with her domestic dictatorship, giving everybody equal opportunity to shine after a White Sale or decent pie baking.

Those women in our small but richy hometown who were lucky enough to be selected as food writer Polly Palmer's Cook of the Week were put on a pedestal, like cakes rising in their sugar petticoats from a crystal stand.

The paper devoted an entire inside page to the gloating these women spouted and the bloating their recipes invariably caused. The staff photographer at the *Daily Times* would bustle into the woman's home and take all sorts of photos of her gadding about her hearth and home.

The words were always sappy and flattering, but none quite as dripping with inflated compliments as the time our town's former *Playboy* centerfold, Tina Ramirez, who'd married a radiologist, wound up Cook of the Week, when everybody and his mama knew the only thing she'd ever greased were her teats poolside at the country club. No way she'd ever plunged those long manicured hands into a tub of Crisco or risked burning her perfect face over a skillet of popping Wesson oil.

Oh, but the story Polly Palmer wrote made her sound like some sort of curvaceous culinary princess. It was the only time the Cook of the Week was photographed lounging by the pool, her 36DDDs oiled like a turkey breast as she lifted in toast her favorite beverage, "Tina's Tornado," a concoction of vodka and liqueur she frothed and then topped with a menacing cone of whipped cream.

"They'll blow you away," the photo caption read beneath Tina's teeny gold bikini. The picture was black and white—it being in the seventies and all—but I'd seen her in that swimsuit and knew it was as gold as the dome on Georgia's capitol building.

"Tina is the quintessential (I had to go look that up, being only 12.) woman, and the kind of goddess and creature of the kitchen and manor we are all just dying to be," Polly gushed in her column. "She's got substance (what Polly meant is money), a great little figure (her knockers) and a set of twins anyone would be proud to call their own."

My sister and I wanted to know if the paper meant her boobies or her wild hellion sons, who always tinkled through the country club fence and right onto the golf course. Those boys were junior devils sent up on a mission of torment. Nobody liked them.

The article went on and on with Polly's blatherings.

"Mrs. Ramirez epitomizes what wife and mother mean, only she takes it much further up the ladder and volunteers as a room parent, was voted 'Sexiest Wife of the Year,' by the VFW Post 352 as well as the Moose Lodge, both in our fair city and two towns south of here in neighboring counties. This is solid evidence of her beauty and far-reaching domestic skills."

My sister and I were curious about the far-reaching skills but we said nothing to our mama.

Polly kept right on bootlicking, and I wanted to take a match to the paper and watch it burn. "Tina and her husband, the renowned radiologist who moved here from Spain, have a home that would put any of Atlanta's mansions to shame. Her décor can leave one rather intimidated, making most of our city's homes look like the stepchildren of her splendidly renovated Victorian mansion on Avondale Heights.

"Tina chooses only the best of the best—be it for her fine dining or her opulent abode."

"'I learned to decorate and choose only the finest at a young age,' says our Cook of the Week while clicking about her enormous kitchen in strappy Prada sandals, one of 388 pairs of designer shoes in her walk-in closet the size of a Wendy's dining room.

"How does she do it?" Polly Palmer asked. "How is it that this knockout and kitchen goddess is able to do it all?

" 'My mother was also a great beauty,' Tina says. 'But she told me being gorgeous doesn't excuse a woman from perfecting her duties in the kitchen and bedroom,' she advised. 'It just gives her more options for dining out.'

"I could not agree more," Polly said right after that quote.

" 'I love reservations,' Tina admitted, 'but one can only choose fine dining so much, if you know what I mean.' She tried to pinch a roll of fat to prove her point, but came up empty-handed since she has the best figure in the entire county, bar none. 'Why skimp when we're talking about our own homes and families?' she asked. 'Why not give them the best of everything?'

"One of Tina's secrets to a happy marriage and home life is she packs her twins' lunch every morning (before returning to her bed for more beauty sleep), providing them with crisp bacon, French toast and real maple syrup in decorative bottles. She tops it off with linen napkins and sterling silver utensils." They love only breakfast for lunch.

"Well, la-de-da," I heard my younger sister say as she read the story and recipes. "Where are the vegetables, Mrs. Ramirez? Where's the fruit Ms. *Playboy* has-been?"

I can still hear Sandy, who couldn't have been more than 10, reading and hissing, flinging words and finally the paper. "Best of everything? How 'bout learning the meaning of the word 'sacrifice' like our poor mother?"

Sandy had made it her mission to fume each time the "Cook of the Week" feature appeared in the paper, seeing all the women's photo layouts as an egregious slight against our own mom, who always said with no conviction in her voice, "Why, that sort of thing doesn't bother me a bit. I'm happy for all the women chosen as Cooks of the Week."

Uh-huh. Right.

"It's one's Christian duty to want nothing but good for others," Mama often said.

So my sister and I took up the cause and decided to rake over the hot grill the women who were selected over our dear mother.

We were purely eaten up with envy as the newspaper plastered our friends' moms on the front of page three, and we had to witness the glaring omission every Wednesday morning when the paperboy threw the rubber-banded news onto our driveway or lawn. I had to endure this for ten or so years, and thought about calling down *Daily Times* and suggesting they come and pay Mama a visit because her spaghetti and Salmon Stew are the best a body could consume, and no one could top her Posse's Hash Sandwiches, perfectly toasted on Colonial's hamburger buns. And, contrary to rumor, our house does NOT buzz as if infested with locusts every night with the sound of an overused electric can opener. Our mama could cook—a little.

She had enough decent meals to toss on the pages of the *Daily Times*, though I knew better than to call Polly Palmer on my Princess telephone and let her have it. Mama would have killed me.

I'd hear my sister mumbling and the papers rattling. "She can't cook her way out of a Piggly Wiggly bag," or "That recipe didn't come from her kitchen. Why, that was Rosemary Hubert's Perfect Peach Cobbler 'cause she made it for me one day and that's all there is to it. You stole it, you lying little witch."

It just plumb tore my sister and me apart every week to see our fine mother passed up yet again as the Cook of the Week, though Mama continued to tell us it didn't matter to her at all.

The week she took to her bed, which is what Southern women do when overcome with life's demands or disappointments, was the Wednesday the Cook of the Week just so happened to be Judy Sue Teeter, who had the perfect daughter named Cassidy way before anyone had that name. Judy Sue's Cassidy came screeching into the world, destined to wear every Little Miss crown ever manufactured.

Judy Sue always got her way and so did Cassidy, a prima donna if there ever was one. "Judy never made anything fresher than a pass at other mamas' husbands," said my sister, who'd seen the woman only in church and really knew nothing about her kitchen capabilities.

Mama was lying like a wounded dog in her bed, pretending she had flu when we assumed it was clearly a case of Passed Over Again Blues. "Sandy, sugar, now that's not the way good Christians talk. I'm sure Judy Sue deserves this attention as much as anyone else."

"Sorry," Sandy said, and continued drawing beards and warts on the photos. "You old bag. Let's see you really cook something for once in your lazy life. What? Can't do it? You just happened to be standing at your gas range like it fell from the sky and you don't know what to do with it?"

"Sandy, that's enough out of you," Mama said. "I'll have to make you write one hundred sentences again, 'I must not make fun of the Cook of the Week.'" She rolled over in bed and didn't say another word for five solid hours, until the clock marched toward six and she knew she had to rise and haul out her pots and pans for mealtime.

We'd tell Mama not to worry and she'd get all mad and say, "I wouldn't be Cook of the Week if they begged me," but we knew differently. She saved recipes and had a special outfit in the closet to wear. Just in case.

While it never happened during our dozen years in that town, the good news is that once we moved away, and after forty-five years of marriage, Mama has finally graduated into a semispectacular cook—give or take a few clunkers here and there.

Her best recipe is still the Salmon Stew she'd make on cold winter nights but was embarrassed to talk about in that small Georgia town. Nobody could ever touch her Creamy Coconut

Cake, but she made it only when it was her turn to host bridge club or attend the bereaved and only if she had the energy. Otherwise, she'd make Mama Dot's Co-Cola Cake, which is really good, but she didn't like using two cake pans and going to all that trouble, so she'd just pour the batter in a big old 9 x 13 casserole dish and serve the black rectangle to all gathered with their cards and coffee cups.

Most of her bridge club was three Bloody Marys to the wind by noon and didn't much care what they ate. And none of them had been a Cook of the Week, either. Well, one had, but Mama forgave her because she was plain sweet and not a bit pretentious and even wore an apron during the photo shoot, while most of the cooks wore their finest threads and had makeovers at the Estée Lauder counter the morning prior.

When you do the math, and figure we lived in that little richy town for twelve years, this comes to 624 women of the 25,000 population who dominated the coveted three-quarter-page spread in the paper while my mother did not.

I heard not long after we moved to Spartanburg, South Carolina, Polly Palmer's people asked, "Whatever happened to that . . . that . . . oh, what's her name? That good-looking tall, thin woman with the two daughters? She might make a fairly decent Cook of the Week."

I don't mean to make Mama sound like she sat on her canned goods and did nothing. This is far from the truth. She worked like an ox at the tasks she enjoyed and excelled at.

It's not her fault she hated cooking and would rather scrub the toilets, mop the floors, make beds, clean windows, service her husband . . . anything but stand over the burning red eyes of her GE range and wonder, "Will this end up a brown meal or an orange one?"

She loved the weekends, her mostly cook-free time, and so did Sandy and I. Friday or Saturday nights meant she and Daddy, then in their 30s, would hit the Moose Lodge or the country club for dining and dancing. It meant a babysitter and either chicken potpies or Totino's Pizzas, both of which cost around a dime back then, and to us tasted pretty near grand. I loved Swanson potpies, the ones with the crust on top and on the bottom. That crust drove me crazy it was so delicious, and I can still smell that bubbling yellow cream oozing up from the dough where Mama had pierced the pies with fork tines so they'd cook faster.

That should say it all. A kid who loves Swanson and Totino's is a child who's born either with no discerning or snobbish palate or whose mom has about as much chance at being Cook of the Week as she does winning the showcase on *The Price Is Right*.

Mom had a repertoire of five to seven meals and when tired, she'd take hot dogs, slice them down the middle as if gutting a fish and stuff the gap with cheddar cheese—a recipe we called "Parched Dogs." This was my least favorite supper, my favorite being taco night served with all the fixings.

On other evenings we'd have Mrs. Paul's Fish Sticks from a box, or pintos and cornbread with a side of onions.

To her credit, Mama turned from Betty Clueless to Betty Crocker on Sundays, fixing marvelous Southern meals such as tender chuck roast cooked in the Crock-Pot, mashed potatoes dripping in butter, homemade gravy and Ford Hook lima beans. She could fry the best chicken—next to my granny's—you've ever eaten, though all Southerners think their own fried chicken beats every other recipe on earth.

The truth is, the ones doing the bragging are all using the same basic recipe and know precisely how hot to get the Crisco and the balance of milk and egg for dunking.

Later we figured out why Mama always cooked her best on Sundays. It was her day of getting some afternoon delight.

"Your father and I are napping," she'd say after taking off her grease-splattered apron and putting away all the Sunday dishes. I can still see her hands, red with the heat of dishwater and shiny from the suds of Palmolive or Dawn. "Our door will be locked so don't come knocking. Y'all run play Barbies or go down to Jane Anne's house."

This tidbit of information is key to uncovering the mysteries of cooking and one of the main reasons women—and men—go to great lengths to prepare scrumptious meals.

It appears that many times, the better the sex or prospect thereof, the better the meal and effort going into it. I know women who'd fly to France and take cooking classes if they were in love and lust enough to try to win a man through his dependence on her Crème Brûlée. Sex and food are about as intertwined as diet and exercise. You do one and expect the other.

Here are a few of Mama's meals to try.

MAMA'S MOST MEMORABLE DISHES

Parched Dogs with Cheese Tongues

Warning: These are strange and, when served to guests, don't go over too well unless the guest is starving, drunk or five years old.

Take a pack of decent-brand hot dogs and slit them from top to bottom.

Stuff with sharp cheddar cheese.

Place on an ungreased cookie sheet and slide in the oven.

Turn oven to Bake 350, cooking until cheese bubbles.

Serve with any canned item in the pantry, along with a tossed salad and at least two cucumber slices, a tomato wedge and Mama's version of Thousand Island Dressing. (See below.)

Pink Paradise Dressing

In a small bowl take some Duke's mayo (the queen of the South's mayonnaise) and ketchup and mix until pink. *Be sure it's true pink. Red means too much ketchup and won't go over too well, nor will Pepto-Bismol pink.*
  If you aim to get fancy, throw in a bit of pickle relish.
  Transfer to a pretty bowl and serve.

Salmon Stew

Sounds gross but this one is truly delicious if you don't mess up and use fat-free milk. That is a big no-no. The key is in the rich milk and a heavy hand on the potatoes and onions. More is better.

Chop up a sweet Vidalia onion or a white onion *(if you can't get your hands on Vidalias).*
  Peel and dice 6 or more Idaho potatoes into bite-size chunks.
  Heat a skillet to medium hot, add butter and sauté the onions until clear.
  In a big pot, boil the potatoes in just enough water to cover them. *(When they're done, there should be a whole bunch of water, and what is there should be nice and starchy-looking.)*
  Now, for the grossest part of the entire process. Take a 15-ounce can of pink salmon and debone it. *(Be careful to remove all the yucky black and silver skins and gooey parts out of it. Give to dog or cat or evil husband/boyfriend.)*
  Then place the chunks of pink meat into the potatoes, adding the onion and butter, and two cans of cream-style corn.
  Next, add a can of evaporated milk, more butter, two cups of regular milk, and salt and pepper. Allow to cook slowly on low to medium heat. Never boil.

If the stew is too thick, add water. *Personally, medium thickness is just right.*

Serve with crusty bread, or if you like being plain, saltines work fine.

This stew is absolutely wonderful for inducing sleep on a cold winter night. And it's great the next day, too.

Not Your Usual Boring Green Bean Casserole

1 can of white shoepeg corn *(a big honking can)*

1 can of French-style green beans. *Get the good kind. Don't try to save 5 cents on a dented generic can.*

Drain all this till it's nearly bone dry. *No one likes a watery casserole.*

½ cup of onion. *In the South, we love our Vidalias.* Chop up the onion. *Nobody likes to get a big nasty piece of onion in her mouth.*

½ cup grated cheddar cheese. *I like the sharp kind. And if you feel adventurous and your heart valves are decent, go ahead and put in ¾ cup instead.*

1½ cans cream of celery soup

½ cup sour cream

Salt and pepper to taste. *Tip: if you add a lot of salt, no one will urinate for days and they will bloat and be unpleasant company.*

1 stick melted butter. *You can use the diet margarine kind, but don't expect it to taste quite as good.*

½ cup finely ground RITZ Crackers. *That's one stack.*

Mix the first seven ingredients together in a large bowl. Pour into a greased 2-quart casserole dish.

Mix melted butter with the RITZ Crackers. Place on top of the green bean and corn mixture.

Bake on 350 for 45 minutes.

You can make this ahead and refrigerate overnight.

This is a vastly improved version of that other green bean casserole you see everywhere, the one with the crunchy dried onions on top.

Ultrafabulous Coconut Cake

1 box white cake mix

1 can Eagle Brand Sweetened Condensed Milk *(Not the diet kind, please!)*

1 can cream of coconut *(Find it where the cocktail mixes are located.)*

1 large tub of Cool Whip

1 package of frozen coconut *(Thaw it.)*

Make cake according to directions on the box.

Pour into a 9 x 13 pan.

When done, pierce the cake top with a fork. Stab the sucker.

Cover the top with the milk and let it soak for about 20 minutes.

Stir cream of coconut and spread over cake.

Add Cool Whip and cover with the coconut so that it looks like an albino porcupine.

Delish!

CHAPTER TWO

Vigilante Grannies' Good Eats and Feats

I thought my Aunt Betty was the only person brave enough or crazy enough to mow down crime, stare it in the face, and do everything in her power to slap Perps and Pervs behind bars.

She became the force to be reckoned with at a lovely lake populated by ducks, children and creeps. She'd drive up as the pervs made out in cars, then flash her lights, zip down the window of her darling Mercedes 450 SL and launch her attack.

"You're sick, did you know that? Do you realize this park is for children and families and not people of your ilk?"

Gosh, I love that word "ilk." It sounds . . . so . . . nasty and ne'r-do-wellish.

"You take that trash somewhere else or I'm dialing 911 on my cell," she'd say, holding up her tiny phone, the bangles on her arm jingling and catching the afternoon sun.

The lake had become a gathering place for gay men still in the closet, many of whom were married and acting AS IF.

"I'm not against gays," Aunt Betty said. "I'm against anyone coming into this family environment and bringing their bedroom business. Now, up the road there are half a dozen motels. I tell them to 'MOVE IT, or I'll dial!'"

Aunt B. is a Vigilante Granny.

Recently, I've come to find out there are other women out

there doing the same thing. My dear friend Mama Dot in Canton, North Carolina, keeps an eye out for lawbreakers, particularly drunks behind the wheel. Her beloved husband was killed by a drunk driver, and since then, Mama Dot has gone from a citizen who chases road punks to a verified graduate of the Civilian Police Academy.

A beautiful, full-figured woman with pink cheeks, an easy smile and dark curly hair, Dorothy Fisher, "Mama Dot," is that unusual combination of tough and tender. "I'm 5'5" and weigh 170 pounds and it's all piss and vinegar," she says.

On the one hand, she can cry during movies, commercials or when someone mentions they have a cold. She even wrote to the man who killed her husband and offered forgiveness and gifts at Christmas.

On the other, she will slam her foot on the accelerator of her maroon Ford Crown Victoria (the same car that police drive) and chase scraggly teens and anybody else she's spotted drinking beer and trying to kill small animals such as possums and squirrels. If a law is broken on the highways and byways of western North Carolina, Mama Dot glows pink, then red, maddening by the minute behind the wheel of her "police" car.

People thought she was a cop long before she got the badge. She had enough attitude to jump out of her car (after running someone down and motioning for them to pull over) to fight crime in a pastel or floral sweater, giant gemstone on every finger and frosted lipstick—giving her that feminine quality. Like I said, she has a heart of gold and fists of steel. She also has a mouth on her that can coo love notes and sweet words galore, or boom up a few notches and scare the wrong-doing out of everyone she encounters.

Recently, she had a big run-in with a trio of teens who were drinking and out for nothing but trouble.

"The first one was a group of cowboys in jacked-up trucks," said Fisher, who considers herself a Vigilante Granny.

"They were coming home and you could see them drinking their beer, passing everything on the road."

Mama Dot witnessed with her own eyes as the driver swerved to the side of the road for the sole purpose of killing a poor little groundhog. She grew livid and her anger boiled as she saw the creature flattened.

"I got behind them and followed them to the Hot Spot," she said. "I parked behind them, blocking them in, and they assumed I was an undercover cop. I've pretty much made a name for myself out here doing this kind of work, and they know I'm not going to put up with it and will sock it to their asses."

She pinned them in with her car, and they shot out of theirs.

"They were all standing with their hands against the truck," Mama Dot said. "I said in a real mean voice, 'You stand right where you are and don't anybody make a move.'"

The driver couldn't control his tongue. "I'm sorry, ma'am. We just got off work and I know it was wrong. We had just opened our beer."

She told them she'd spent the past few years paying close attention to drunk drivers and let them know how her husband had died when a sloshed young man behind the wheel of his car ran her husband's rig off the side of the interstate and into a ravine. "Let me tell you I don't believe for one minute you just opened that beer."

"Ma'am," one of the guys said, "I just got out of jail. Please don't write me a ticket."

Mama Dot, a former flight nurse paramedic and Civil Rights activist, surveyed the beer container and realized there weren't many gone. She'd give them a slight break. "OK," she said. "I'm going to tell you boys something. You're going to be with me on this. And I want to know what possessed you to run over that little innocent groundhog?"

"It was just a groundhog," one of the hoodlums said.

"No, no, no." Mama Dot wasn't about to let up. "It could have been a child. Even if it had been a possum, I'd still be mad at you."

The trio tried to think of something to say. "We've just always done stuff like that," one admitted.

"Well, starting today, you're going to quit hitting them," Mama Dot said, her hands on her hips and her "mean cop" face in place. "I must have scared the crap out of them," she said later.

She spread her stance wide and squared off with the teens. "We're going to go back and get that groundhog and anything else dead in that vicinity, then we're going to give it a proper burial."

Mama Dot, who's beat the skin off two abusive husbands (not necessarily her own), said one of the tough guys was about to cry. "We shouldn't have killed that groundhog," he said, all trembly-voiced. "You are 100 percent right."

"You should leave all God's creatures alone. Listen, I don't have all day to fool with this. You get in the truck and do not try anything funny because my car can outrun your hoopty mobile any day of the week. You better obey all traffic laws because I'm watching. Set that beer on the sidewalk before we go."

Mama Dot and her troop of tipsy groundhog killers then returned to the scene of the crime. "I was glued to their bumper," she said, "and they were giving signals and doing so nicely."

Once back at the murder scene, Mama Dot put on her hazard lights and parked behind the truck on the side of the road.

"I made them get out and pick up the little groundhog," she said, "and there was a dried-up possum near the site, so I made them get that, too."

Mama Dot ordered them over to a grassy area away from the highway traffic. "You dig anywhere around here and you dig deep," she said. She noticed some rather large tree limbs down. "Go to your truck and get some rope," she said. "You can make a cross out of these branches so that every time you drive by you'll remember what you did and think the eyes of God are on you. I'll be checking periodically to see if it's still there."

They did as told, and she followed the young men back to the convenience store and made them promise not to ever drink and drive or hit small animals.

"It may sound harsh to you," she said, "but like I said, a drunk driver killed my husband and he was the finest human being on this planet."

Since then, Mama Dot, the Vigilante Granny, has seen the fellows quite a few times.

"Mrs. Fisher," they often say, "we don't try to kill possums or anything on the road anymore."

"That's good," she said. "Keep your eyes out. I'll be patrolling these roads, you hear?" They listened, too, because every so often she sees a fresh cross marking the site where a groundhog lost his life to rebel-rousing drunks.

Looking back on everything, she was pleased with how she handled the boys.

"The only thing I wished I'd done was make them pray."

Drunks aren't the only target of Mama Dot's crime-busting rants. The other day she saw a man spitting on the sidewalk and had a pure, all-out fit.

"He was crossing the street, then leaned against the wall and worked hard to get a big hawker up," she said.

"YOU KNOW YOU DON'T DO THAT!" she shouted.

"Who you?" he asked, grammar needing an overhaul.

"I'm the bitch who's gonna knock you out if you don't clean that up."

The phlegm, a gruesome shade of bodily breakdown, oozed on the concrete. She handed him a box of baby wipes and watched until he'd scrubbed every inch of the sidewalk.

As with most of her "victims," he also thought she was a cop.

Soon, she plans to get deputized because in her words, "I want a ticket book and to be able to carry a gun."

"I'm looking for any infraction of the rules," she said one

afternoon, biting into a steak fry. "I'm going to be out there looking for things."

Here are her "Women Over 50 Rules to Live By," her "RECIPE," she said, that's much better for the soul than food is. When asked to give a favorite dish, she gave this gem of advice instead:

"A whole new chapter of my life is now opening, and can for you, too. You've raised your family, done stuff by the book, and now it's time to do what you want.

"Let your hair down, let it blow in the wind. Go dancing, pull your skirt above the knees. If you've never worn a pair of shorts, get a pair.

"Stay busy, get involved in community service. Don't think retirement means sitting home and vegetating. Get up and out there and do what you've always wanted to do but didn't have time or were scared to try."

Another Vigilante Granny, besides my Aunt Betty and Mama Dot, is a woman named Deb Lockhart. This registered nurse tends the sick by day and chases crime by night.

Deb Lockhart of Enka, North Carolina, tells of her run-in with crime, using plenty of verbs and adjectives—a yarn spun with bravery and an estrogen overload.

She was on her way to her mother's house in Hendersonville, North Carolina, a few weeks ago when all kinds of chaos broke loose at a four-way traffic light in the Enka area.

"Our stoplight hadn't changed to green, so everybody was kind of waiting at the four-way," said Lockhart, a recovery room nurse, mother and grandmom. She noticed a Toyota Corolla sitting to her left and saw firsthand a Chevy four-wheeler plowing into the Corolla's rear end, sending it spinning into the intersection.

She looked over at the truck and had a thought. "That guy's going to run."

Sure enough, he whipped a 180 and took off down Brevard

Road, digging into the concrete with a bad and barely drivable wheel.

On his tail, Lockhart pressed her accelerator in full pursuit, never mind she was carting around her daughter and brand-new grandbaby. She made sure they were buckled in safely and then went about her Vigilante Granny business.

She jotted down the license plate and called the highway patrol from her cell phone. She clicked on her flashers so other motorists would realize she was a woman who meant business. When the hit-and-run man turned into a car dealership, she stayed right with him.

Lockhart squeezed her eyes to get a good gander at him and pointed to his tag and her cell phone, trying to let him in on a little secret: "Gotcha!" she mouthed.

"He looked me dead in the face and took off," she said. "This one wasn't getting away. We followed him down Brevard Road and he turned left onto Pole Creasman Road." She was right behind him, even when he veered into a construction area, his radiator beginning to steam.

"His radiator finally gave up and he couldn't go any farther," she said. "He got out of his truck and took off running up a hill all drunk and wobbling."

Like all decent vigilante grannies, Lockhart peeped into his glove box and scribbled on paper all the pertinent information. She called the highway patrol again, then got back in her car, knowing the guy would have to come over the hill. When he did, she was waiting for him at the Hot Spot.

"He went straight for the pay phone, and I got out and stood where he was making the phone call," she said. "I was on the phone to the highway patrol, saying, 'We've got your hit-and-run fellow right here.'"

In the end, the guy was charged with Driving While License Revoked and hit-and-run, according to Lisa Patton, an office assistant with the highway patrol.

Lockhart said she joked and asked for her own deputy badge.

"I want to be deputized," she said. "They (the cops) were busy laughing at the relentless grandmother and her posse. They were amused."

Lockhart said that while her daughter thinks she's nuts and advised her not to tell this story publicly, she has no regrets.

"I'd do it again in a heartbeat," she said.

It certainly beats sitting on the other side of the law, and she knows from personal experience what it feels like to squirm in the back of a patrol car. Like Mama Dot's husband, Deb was the victim of a hit-and-run driver, though she obviously survived.

When the incident occurred, Deb had just had some "female surgery," and was wearing a garment that allowed her to "de-Velcro" the crotch with rapidity.

"I felt like an old-lady stripper every time I ripped it open to pee," she said.

Before the hit-and-run occurred, she and her posse were in search of a potty stop and Deb's Velcro was open.

"When the lawman asked me to sit in his backseat to file the report, the scanner was making so much noise that he requested I move over to the center of the seat so he could hear me." After he'd asked his questions, Deb noticed her pantyliner, which she wore to prevent contact with the Velcro, had adhered to the seat she had scooted away from.

She felt her face heat up and her heart quicken its beats. "The guy was looking at me, and I was unable to just snatch it up with my hand, so as I climbed out of the cruiser, I was trying to kind of pinch it up with a Kegel—an ass-crunch maneuver—thinking if I had spent some time with the ThighMaster, I might have been better equipped to save myself some embarrassment.

"I got tickled," she said, "and then came the uncontrollable laughter and I could not get out of the squad car," Deb said. "The cop finally asked me if I was on drugs, which pushed me over the edge. I'd been driving seventeen hours and was ill-equipped to demonstrate any self-control."

Long story short, Deb did manage to rescue the wayward minipad, using her butt cheeks, and all ended well.

Nell's Best Original Jell-O Pie

"It's my mom's Original Jell-O Pie, she developed herself over sixty-three years ago," Mama Dot, the civilian cop, said.

Makes 2 pies.

1 package of Jell-O, any flavor
1 cup sugar
3 cups pineapple juice (1 small can, unsweetened)
2 beaten eggs
1 pint cream (whipped) (Can use Cool Whip.)
2 graham cracker crusts

Mix first four ingredients together; bring to a boil.
Cool.
Add whipped cream.
Pour into two pie plates lined with graham cracker crust.
Chill well and serve.

This is the best pie you will ever eat and your kids will love it, Mama Dot promises.

CHAPTER THREE

Erotic Eating: When Love and Food Collide

It's not that hard to figure out. A lot of men love to see women eat.

Cooking and sex are so closely linked I'm not sure which came first. All I know is that at least on some occasions, men and women both cook in order to get love and/or sex, and that it all starts when a girl is old enough to date and a boy takes her to eat and expects kissing or heavy petting after he pays the restaurant tab and tip.

I always know when my husband hauls me to the Red Lobster (his favorite place), which I call Redneck Lobster, he expects adult entertainment when we get home.

I've yet to understand how a man stuffed with shrimp and fried clams could think of anything but lying on the couch in a semicoma bloated from all that food. Apparently, it doesn't work that way for them. Men could be on their hospice beds, oxygen tubes hanging out of their noses along with the unclipped hairs and death's intravenous drip coursing through their bloodstreams, and still . . . the sheet begins to rise.

You can always tell that sex and eating are linked if you just listen to the audible clues, the foremost being the moaning after each bite. When you hear someone you love moaning during one of your meals, it's about the best foreplay you could imagine. Kitchen virgins who don't cook well enough to get the moan factor, typically go for take-out and then repackage it in their CorningWare as if they'd prepared it themselves.

While I don't want my mama and daddy reading this next passage, I felt it my duty to include it to show how powerful food can be as an aphrodisiac. I was going to wait until my folks died to share this, but instead, I'll write it and tell them it was all made up. But it's really true.

It was my fortieth birthday and my husband and I had gone to Carrabba's Italian Grill (which he thinks is highly overrated and I think is absolutely delicious). We then went to the mall to exchange my birthday present, which had started out an opal bracelet, but I told him only women in nursing homes wear opals, which is how I ended up a with a beautiful garnet and diamond bracelet that sparkles and shines and really is glamorous. Garnets are a poor woman's ruby. Just as pretty!

I must say opals are fine. Fine, if you are in seventh grade and the first boy you've ever French-kissed gets you one for Christmas. They are also OK if you are 80 years old and have one of those wet, waddling necks, dusted with baby powder for church and hot afternoons. Not that there's a thing wrong with wobbling powdered necks or opals. I'm just not one for either.

Back to the big fortieth birthday evening.

"I wanna do something a wee bit kinky," I say to my husband postdinner, realizing he rarely gets action, unless it's from someone I don't know about. When you're married with two kids and two careers and two different shifts, it's hard to fit it in. Sex, that is.

I was guilted into being a kinky sex kitten by *REDBOOK* magazine, which is always telling women how to send their partners to Mars by way of rocket-force sex. I hate those magazines that put all the work in our shoes. I don't need some 25-year-old underpaid intern for Hearst magazines telling me how to give the best . . . you know what.

"Kinky?" my ever-skeptical husband asked. "What are you up to now besides falling asleep right after supper?"

Going home would mean putting kids to bed and brushing teeth, hearing some major whining and carrying on, and then being too tired to even think about the mattress mambo. One never knows what might transpire once the kids are transported from sitter to home. They could fall asleep or be WIDE-awake, meaning no chance of home-turf Hanes surfing.

"Let's just turn in here and do it in the back of the van," I said as we traveled the road toward home, also the path that leads to Pleasant Hill Memorial Gardens, a mountaintop burial ground that boasts absolutely breathtaking views of the long-range vistas. "Whip it over there."

"The cemetery? Are you out of your mind?"

"I'm 40. It's dark. When you're 40 and it's dark, it's OK to have sex in a cemetery or anywhere else you choose."

He gave it a half-second's thought (men could not care less about location, as long as they're promised sex treats), then found a spot on a knoll. One thing led to another until we were in the backseat and my husband unfastened and hurled the youngest's car seat out into the tombstones for more you-know-what room. The car seat thumped and thudded and landed somewhere down the hill near a family mausoleum.

At that point, I tried to remember the rules of REDBOOK's steamy sex guide and attacked my husband as if I were a teenager with raging hormones.

"Whoa!" he said. "This isn't the Kentucky Derby. I want to keep my teeth for as long as possible."

We go at it for a while, windows fogging and the smell of fried clams like a seafood veil, and I can't help but notice a headstone and a little red-white-and-blue American flag bobbing up and down in my line of vision. Hard to concentrate on the "bidness" when I keep seeing the flag and the grave and the big old full moon like a disapproving eye.

When it was all over with, and quite fun, I might add, I stepped out of the van and into the cold, moony night to at least introduce myself to the fellow underground who kept entering into my peripheral vision during the Act. I stared at the letters etched into the granite and Lord help, of all the thousands of graves in that cemetery, there he was. John Fields Williams III, dead two years and one month and husband of a beloved former coworker.

"Sorry about that, John," I mumbled and hopped in the van laughing like some newly middle-aged woman who hadn't been serviced in a month and finally gets nookied in a cemetery.

Cemetery sex, people. Give it a whirl after a nice seafood dinner. There's something erotic about doing it in a land where no one else has a pulse. I'm sure it's a fetish, but dang! It's a hot one.

I think about that fortieth birthday night a lot, though it's only been six years ago. When you've been married twenty years and don't have too much sex, it's easy to live on the fumes of your last interesting tango.

I'd read this book that came to the office about being a domestic diva and utilizing all furnishing and housewares as possible tools of seduction including the kitchen tile or linoleum. I'm sorry, but I have a bad back and cold tile does it no good. Neither will I become scorching hot while writhing near my range. Just looking at the two pitiful burners and missing Jenn-Air pieces leaves me shaken and frigid.

The domestic diva book mentioned food, too, and said women should practice the art of "Seductive Mastication and Digestion." Certain foods have long been known for their aphrodisiac properties, but did you realize, too, that it's not necessarily what you eat but how you eat it?

Think of that scene in *Flashdance* where the couple is eating lobster and the woman is wearing nothing but a large bib and can't stop licking her fingers while her chocolate-drop eyes bore into her hunky man-prey.

If someone bites on my idea for a TV show, *Bon Appe-Cheat* or *Cheatin' and Eatin'*, I plan to include romance tips along with cooking suggestions.

Dining in front of the opposite sex is an art form and one that has its own set of guidelines and rules of etiquette. Few things could be more romantic and seductive than taking a woman to dinner and her throwing out all neuroses concerning Atkins and South Beach and just enjoying the living daylights out of her food.

Why, men have eaten like Neanderthals for years. Turnabout is fair and sexy play.

I decided to try this Erotic Eating on a completely attached and utterly in-love-with-another-woman dinner companion. Mercy laws . . . He all but swooned with every bite I took. We were good friends, otherwise I couldn't have used him for practice, plus I warned him: "I plan to eat my food as if I'm making love to each morsel."

"Whatever you need to do," was his casually cool reply.

Halfway through my meal, this poor man had sweat beads pooling on his brow and it was 14 degrees outside. "You gotta come over and teach my wife how to eat," he said. "Damn."

So, listen up sex-deficit sisters. Here's the deal. When you go to a seafood restaurant, order the crab claws and learn how to open them before you arrive so you don't look like Rowan Atkinson crunching through crustaceans in the movie *Mr. Bean's Holiday*. Perfect your skills with the crab cracker or learn to snap the claw by hand in precisely the right spot to release long and succulent strips of pure white crab. The meat will emerge from the shell ready for a buttery skinny-dip.

Go ahead and express your hot desires for food. Eating with lust is as erotic as wearing a thong teddy from Victoria's Secret.

I rushed to phone Mama with these thoughts and ideas, figuring she'd call me a big fat harlot.

"Oh, sweetie, I never told you about eating in front of men. You can't moan and go all out because they'll think you're a hussy. Your Aunt Hattie used to drive them all wild 'cause she couldn't help herself at the table. She would grunt and groan and carry on about every bite she took, and she not only cleared a table but could also empty a room. It was a complete embarrassment, especially if you gave her a vine-ripe tomato that dripped juices down her chin."

With this in mind, all ye women afraid to swallow food in front of a man, take heart and EAT! No need to play coy or say, "I'm on a diet. I'll just have a salad with no dressing."

That's not sexy. That's neurotic. Nothing worse than a woman on a date ordering a dry salad and Diet Coke. You can imagine the messages this sends men: "I'm cold and frigid." "I only like sex when I'm not feeling fat, which is hardly ever." "I have hang-ups about everything in life, including eating."

If a woman wants to impress a mate or lay out a scene for seduction, she'll set the table and get down to the business of cooking something grand and sort of greasy.

A negligee is no competition for a perfect lasagna and loads of mozzarella dribbling from the lips of a lover. A bustier is no match for a meal of crab claws dipped in hot melted butter and running down one's jaw.

People like Aunt Jemima, Julia Child and Betty Crocker must have gotten plenty of action on their Sertas because no one could possibly enjoy slaving over a hot stove unless a major reward was attached.

Just as a meal can be erotic, dining with someone new or a stranger is often as embarrassing as stripping in a junior high gym class.

The act of eating is personal, sensual, and has spawned countless books on the proper way to break bread in mannerly ways. A napkin in the lap is just a start.

A few years ago, I was part of a national fund-raiser called "Lunch with a Leader." Those chosen as "leaders" were auctioned on eBay, and the highest bidder was treated to a lunch date with the local, regional or national celebrity.

It was a cold January morning when North Carolina's "Lunch with a Leader" kicked off, featuring some of our state's notables such as actors, educators, lawmakers, musicians, even race car drivers willing to donate their time and lunch money, all for a good cause.

Big names like NASCAR star Bill Elliott and sports stand-outs Dell Curry and Jake Delhomme went up for bid to bene-fit Communities In Schools—a program to help students learn and stay on track and, pretty much not drop out and get on crack.

For some odd or desperate reason (maybe not enough real stars could donate a decent lunch) my mug flashed on the eBay website, and a sweetheart of a gentleman with no criminal record bid high enough (mere pennies compared to what ac-tress Linda Hamilton reeled in) to eat lunch with me.

My mother still can't understand why anyone would pay to dine with her daughter, but I told her it was for a good cause and to just let it go, which, of course, she did not. Instead, she became fixated and concerned about my upcoming lunch, and her thoughts on the matter swelled and stewed.

After six months of planning, Howard the Innkeeper, my high bidder, picked me up on his BMW motorcycle for an hour's drive on the Blue Ridge Parkway followed by a lunch of his choice. I was to buy the meal and throw in a couple of my books that had yet to wind up at the Goodwill.

My mama, always ready to jump at an opportunity to lec-ture and nag, began her phone and e-mail campaign as quickly as the bidding ended.

"I saw where someone paid $255 to eat with you," she wrote, her voice registering the kind of shock one usually re-serves upon learning her spouse has cheated with a 19-year-old wanna-be immigrant, or announced his until-then-hidden gayness.

"I know whoever ends up with you sitting across from them will never forget it. I should have sent you to finishing school when I had the chance. Listen up. You can review the basics, since it's too late to send you a manners coach. For starters, chew with your mouth closed and use your napkin often. It's not to blow your nose with. Remember, that's unacceptable even for those with sinus problems. Don't reach up and pick your nose, either. I've seen you do that without even realizing it."

I kid you not, these were her words, and here I am old enough to be a grandmother.

Mama continued, as she is prone to do in e-mails when I can't interrupt her or hang up the phone. "Let that poor man who spent all his money have a chance to talk a tad," she advised, "and don't eat spinach. Be sure and order something soft. You know how meat can fly off a plate and land in strange places.

"Try not to put on lipstick at the table," she went on, knowing her daughter all too well. "And don't look around the room too much. You remember your wedding day when you couldn't even focus on your husband or the preacher 'cause you were too busy periscoping around to see who showed up for your big day? You also need to be sure and sit up straight. You know how you tend to slump. Also, we wouldn't want your boobs on the table, now, would we? That's trashy. They're much too big for my taste, and it's best you wear a roomy blazer to hide the things."

She was on a roll, my mother, and believe me, if it had been a phone conversation, I'd have hung up three paragraphs ago. She must have forgotten to take her hormones.

"Tell your 'bad' side to stay home," she said. "Most important, be sure and say a blessing for the food and the children. All gifts we receive in life are from God. He will be glad you used yours to help these schoolchildren, and he will be thrilled if you cover up those big boobs with a giant blazer."

That was Mama's precious two-cents' worth, and why I love

her so much. I tried to do everything she advised during my lunch date with Howard Dusenbery, the innkeeper. I couldn't have asked for a nicer lunch companion or one more well mannered and good at conversation. Innkeepers are quite known for their upscale manners and probably read lots of books on etiquette since their livelihood depends upon it.

As we made our way through Greek salads topped with tender chicken, the lunch seemed to fly by. I picked up the tab and left the tip.

Handing Howard a couple of autographed books, I noticed him trying not to look at part of my face. You know what I mean? Like when someone has a bum eye and you do all you possibly can to not look in that eye? That's what Howard was doing to my mouth.

I ran my tongue across my teeth and felt a bump, a clump.

"Excuse me, Howard. It seems I've dropped something under the table." I hated to lie, especially since this was a charity and involved children's educations and not living lives on crack and meth, and forged 'scripts of Vicodin.

I dove down with my purse and dug in my vast dark, cavernous bag for a mirror. As I squatted under the linen tablecloth, with just enough light to see, I spotted a chunk of spinach in my teeth.

It had been there at least five very long minutes, which meant lots of words had been exchanged between Howard and me, and he'd had the misfortune of trying to pry his eyes away from my green blob—the Incredible Mr. Baby Hulk in my teeth. It must have taken great effort.

I reached for my eyebrow tweezers and plucked the spinach free before rising back up and into my seat.

"How's the scenery down there?" Howard asked, bemused.

"Better than the scenery you had to see in my teeth."

"I figured you'd see it sooner or later," he said. "Didn't bother me a bit."

Perhaps I'd eaten with sex-propelled gusto. Maybe some Greek salad dressing dribbled down my chin in an erotic fashion. Maybe my chewing style seemed nothing less than a slow pole dance.

Or maybe Howard the Innkeeper just didn't care.

Here are a couple of easy recipes my dear and precious double-virgin-prior-to-marriage mama says will light any man's fire and desire. Only she'd never use the words "fire" and "desire." The last recipe in this chapter is from Wild Aunt Betty. She guarantees the results of her cake nothing short of physical fireworks.

Pay Dirt

1 woman
1 small boxed gift *(perhaps a diamond engagement ring)*
1 small store-bought cake
1 bended knee
1 delicious kiss
Slice the cake into two layers.
Scoop out the middle of the bottom layer.
Put the boxed gift there and bury it with the top layer and icing.
Have the woman slice the cake.
When she hits "pay dirt," hit the floor on bended knee.
Prepare for that delicious kiss.

The Ultimate Steak Dinner

1 woman
2 tenderloin steaks
2 spinach salads
2 nonalcoholic drinks *(Not drinking booze will impress her and help you rise to the occasion later. No, my mother didn't say that part about "rising.")*

Dressing

Mix together:
1 cup salad oil
¼ cup white vinegar
⅓ cup ketchup
1 small onion, grated
2 tsp. Worcestershire sauce
Top with real bacon, boiled eggs and fresh mushrooms

"If the woman has spinach in her teeth, don't tell her,"
Mama says, "Instead, tenderly remove it with a toothpick."

Multiple Orgasms Cake

My Aunt Betty's romance recipes are a lot steamier than
Mama's, because Aunt B. never had that fear of admitting to hot
passion. Here is her famous (among certain enlightened circles) cake.
"Guaranteed to work," she said.

1 box white cake mix
2 cups powdered sugar
2 (8-oz.) packages cream cheese, softened
2 packages frozen strawberries, thawed and well drained
1 large and 1 medium container Cool Whip
1 carton of fresh strawberries
Blueberries (optional)

Add lots of love.
Bake three layers, thin layers, according to package directions.
Cool the cake.
Mix powdered sugar with cream cheese in the mixer on medium until fluffy.

Spread this on first cake layer.

Spread frozen strawberries on top of the cream cheese.

Stir both containers of Cool Whip with spoon until fluffy.

Spread a layer of Cool Whip on top of the strawberries.

Continue with second cake layer: cream cheese, strawberries, Cool Whip.

Same with top cake layer.

Now spread Cool Whip all over the cake.

Garnish with halved fresh strawberries, dusted in real sugar.

If you prefer, you can add blueberries.

CHAPTER FOUR

Once You've Done a Meal, You Have to Be Dead to Get Out of Another

About a decade ago I collapsed at my desk. It wasn't one of those glamorous Southern swoonings, but more like an ostrich losing its footing, squawking as it falls to the ground. Coworkers ceased their typing for a moment, then quickly returned to the task at hand.

In a newsroom, it's not all that unusual for one of us to topple and completely fall apart. Such is the nature of the business when deadlines are involved and editors' demands are shouted over the din of clacking keyboards and deafening phone conversations.

It was just after 5 PM the day I keeled over. I was sitting there feeling fine, waiting on a paycheck and for people to return my calls. I'd eaten a big lunch, and hours later put in maybe ten minutes on a treadmill, which for me is as good as it gets.

It's funny how you can be in perfect health, then suddenly something washes right over you, signaling imminent death. This is exactly what happened as my hands tingled and went numb, followed by a battery-acid taste in my mouth. I knew right then, this was IT. It was my time to meet Jesus, or the other fellow. Only I wasn't ready because people were counting on me to provide a meal, my first that included in-laws and expectations.

"Tracy," I sputtered weakly, beseeching the kind spirit of the young woman seated across from me. "Call 911. I'm dying."

Tracy Mixson was a copy editor who had first aid training and once even drove to Florida to help Hurricane Andrew victims. She rushed over and took my pulse and dialed an ambulance. It seemed she was on the phone a long time answering too many questions.

"She's in her 30s. That's right. Eggplant Parmesan for lunch . . . Yes . . . A pink Flintstones vitamin, a prescription for sleep problems."

"Get off the phone," I demanded, as only the dying have a right to do. For some reason, I forgot that dispatchers aren't the ones who actually get in the ambulance and race to the scene. I imagined them asking Tracy questions while the clock ticked away precious moments of my life. "Please! Get off the phone so they can get here faster."

Mixson remained calm and efficient, flicking away long strands of her straight black hair. "They're sending a crew, Susan. Calm down. It's not who's on the phone that's coming. Breathe into this bag and you'll quit twitching."

As another attack swooped, she held my hand and talked me into staying alert. And alive. Breathe in the bag, hear it crinkle; breathe out, watch it inflate, until a moment later it was over and I felt fine, even a bit stupid. I was, in my mind, a ridiculous woman.

"Call them back and tell them not to come. It was probably just a panic attack." I knew that's what it was because I had had one ten or so years before while working as a news intern after the psycho coroner had shown me a severed hand floating in a bucket at the morgue.

"Really, Tracy. Call them back, OK?"

But it was too late, and sirens screamed as if a fire raged or a robbery was in progress or a bear was stuck in a tree somewhere in our fair city. No one would have thought such a shrill cry for help was for a silly woman with lipstick up to her nose and high heels flung under a desk. Rather than for a woman more worried about the pot roast cooking at home than about her blood sugar levels and potentially fatal EKGs. Rather than for a woman thinking, "Will English peas go with the roast or would limas taste better?"

The entire attack had been the direct result of buying a chuck roast on sale for $1.49 a pound and then breaking out the Crock-Pot and tossing in some Lipton's Onion Soup Mix and water. These were the actions of an overconfident woman who should have stuck to Tuna Helper with potato chips on top for extra zip.

A day of light mania had pushed forth the confidence to ask my in-laws to dinner, and now all I could think about was the chuck roast and whether it was shriveling to the size of a burned biscuit. Would it serve four? Would the corners turn in like bad toenails?

I had been married for years, but cooked for my husband's parents only on occasion. One memorable one being my zucchini lasagna, which didn't go over well with my father-in-law, who plucked out all the zucchini slices and stacked them like a tower on his plate, explaining, "I don't eat cucumbers."

My time to have them to dinner again was long overdue, and I knew if I went to the hospital they would think I was trying to get out of doing the cooking. That's what I would think if I had a daughter-in-law and she asked me to dinner and then she suddenly called out of the blue complaining of a heart attack while at her workplace.

I'd think, "Hmm. She doesn't have a bad heart. She just isn't up to cooking. Why, faking heart attacks to get out of serving a meal is the oldest trick in the book."

The thought was interrupted by a team of six men in uniforms rushing into the building holding giant orange medical boxes by their sides.

"Go tell them to wait in the hall, Tracy. I don't want them

stomping in here and causing a commotion. Everybody already thinks I'm a freak."

"You could be in the midst of a myocardial infarction," she said. "You've got to take these seriously, Susan. My cousin had one and is now wearing a pacemaker and is never far from the defib paddles. He can't get anywhere near a microwave or he'll explode."

"I need to put on some lipstick," I said, not wanting to hear about bodily hardware and electrical jump-starting. After a few moments of rummaging around on the floor, I found my purse, reapplied a coat and recovered my shoes.

"Tell the PMS people I'll meet them in the snack shop."

"EMS. EMS people," Tracy said. "Listen, it's no big deal. You've already caused one scene, but I'll take them to the snack bar so try to make it there without incident. Take the elevator, not the stairs."

I walked into the room, *clackety-clacking* and smiling with big rust-colored lips. They asked tough questions.

"Do you know what day of the week it is?"

"Do you know what year this is?"

For a while, I said nothing. Finally, I answered. "It's Tuesday, the 20th century, BC," wanting, but not daring to add, "And I've got a roast drying to shreds in my Crock-Pot because I forgot to throw in a cup of water."

They escorted me to an ambulance, checked vitals and pricked my finger. About twenty minutes later they had me hooked to an EKG machine, one of them no doubt seeing and checking out my dirty and tattered bra with the underwires springing out like metal tongues from the cups. They read wavy pieces of paper that showed my heartbeats zooming up and down like rows of mountains.

"You've got some PVCs," one said.

"Huh?"

"PVCs. Quite a run of them."

"Aren't those pipes you use to install toilets?"

"Preventricular contractions," another said, smiling. "Irregular heartbeat. Anything happening that would have brought this on?"

Well, let's see. "I'm having the in-laws for dinner. I'm not much of a cook, see, and my roast is drying to kibble. I'm sure by the time I get home and serve the thing, my kin will need to grow another row of teeth just to bite through it. That or a chainsaw."

The kind crew suggested we go to the hospital for further testing, but I said there was no way in the world I had time to go.

"If I don't serve that roast tonight . . . this very night . . . you can't possibly understand the consequences, the talk that will occur behind my back. See, my in-laws don't think I do a damn thing but bring home McDonald's every night for the family or live off the Tuna and Hamburger Helpers. This was my chance to show them I do know my way around one or two kitchen devices."

"Well, your heart is—"

"My heart will absolutely shut down all valves if I don't serve some beef to a certain set of carnivores tonight. I promise to call the cardiologist tomorrow for an appointment."

Reluctantly, they radioed in to the hospital to pretty much say they'd wasted a trip and priceless gas on a woman who clearly had no intentions of seeing the inside of the ER.

"Patient refuses transport," they said.

"I'm sorry," I told them. "I hope you don't get a commission on how many you bring in."

I couldn't tell them the real reason I didn't want "transport." How can you explain to men in uniform and draped in lifesaving devices that a Southern woman planning dinner for in-laws is NOT going to check herself into the local hospital?

I signed a waiver and hurried home to boil a bag of MINUTE Rice, put on a pot of Ford Hook limas and douse my dried but edible roast in water, hoping it would bloat a bit.

Because I managed to pull off this meal, even serving it with a Sara Lee cheesecake that had them all raving, it was only fitting they chose me to take over the Thanksgiving holiday meal, a torch they'd been dying to pass for at least half a dozen years. Who could blame them? There comes a time when no one over 60 wants to do every holiday meal, thus they hunt for someone to take on the enormous task.

Looking back, I should have allowed transport to the nearest emergency room and let the roast disintegrate.

DINNER FOR THE IN-LAWS

Crock-Pot Roast

Buy a chuck roast: Make sure to get a lean one unless you like fat. Also make sure it's large because they shrink substantially during cooking.

Put the roast in the Crock-Pot on slow, all-day cooking. Usually 6–8 hours, unless one has to spend time in an ambulance or another unforeseen emergency situation. *Remember, the longer it cooks, the more it will shrivel up. So don't be cheap. Spend the extra two dollars on a larger cut of meat.*

Add at least two cups of water and one pack of Lipton's Onion Soup Mix.

Flip the roast if you're around. If not, have someone do the flipping for you.

Rolls

Buy a bag of whole wheat rolls *(unless your kin are like some of mine and believe God created wheat solely to make white bread.)*

Limas

Buy a bag of Ford Hook limas, the extra large beans. Or if eating limas the size of small mice isn't appetizing, buy the baby limas.

Cook both for a long time. Season with butter, salt and pepper. *(Southerners don't like things unless they mush in their mouths.)*

Dessert

Visit your grocer's frozen food section and choose anything you can just thaw out.

CHAPTER FIVE

If the Baby Comes Early, Blame It on the Ham

I'd always assumed that if you took on one holiday meal, you'd never have to volunteer for another. I was wrong. If the kin die off and Heaven takes some of the best cooks, it leaves the family no choice but to divvy up the remaining holiday meals.

Easter went to me, even though I was 8.9 months pregnant and with major complications that included another case of Irritable Uterus Syndrome, a condition in which the ute contracts as if having temper tantrums and threatens to toss out a baby way before it's due.

No matter. The folks had digested a couple of turkey meals and a pot roast or two, so later I got the big hint to take on the Easter ham.

It went down the way Thanksgiving did.

"Oh, mercy," a relative who shall remain unnamed said. "I got this bad hip giving me fits and can't even take my own garbage to the road. I can't even go downstairs to wash a load of clothes so if you smell something, it's probably me."

Or here's another one I heard from a different set of kin. "We've pretty much given up on the Easter meal. I reckon your daddy and I will be fine having a pimiento cheese sandwich after church that day. We ate tacos last Christmas Eve, so I guess as long as we tell Jesus we're His and recognize the day as one to glorify His rising, it doesn't matter if we have a pack of Nabs and a Diet Coke. It's all the same. We'll just say a longer prayer."

This side of the family tree knows I can't bear to hear of people eating the wrong foods on holidays; it must all match up. Turkey goes with Thanksgiving and ham with Easter and Christmas. Not a pack of Nabs or a pimiento cheese sandwich.

If there's one thing I'm not going to do it's let a holiday UP and die just because someone has decided to UP and quit cooking it.

"I'll do Easter," I said, having no control over my mouth or what spewed forth. "All of you come over." This very sentence led to my permanent post in the calendar year and not a one-time thing.

"But you're pregnant," they faintly protested.

"There's nothing on the hams that spout warnings to pregnant women. It's not like a fifth of liquor." How hard could it be? A 10-pound pig's ass? A little cheating such as buying the potato salad and rolls? If taking over Easter would please these wonderful kin, then I'd do it, despite the fact I'd never cooked a ham in my life and had no clue what it would be like or if it'd have guts tucked up in the anus cavity like the turkeys did.

"Well, honey," they all cooed, "you really don't have to do this. I mean, look. You're pregnant and the doctor said if you got out of bed you could deliver too early."

"It's OK. I'll do it in shifts. I'll throw in the ham and then go lie down for a day or two. I'll chop eggs for six hours and then rest for seven."

By the time the big Easter Feast arrived at my home on the hill, I was in the throes of early labor, and trying to hold it back was like playing tug-of-war with a dozen elephants.

It's all that fat ham's fault. Gwaltney, $1.88 per pound for the spiral-cut, honey-glazed version at Ingles. I don't even like

ham, but you wouldn't have known it to look in my grocery
cart the day before Easter Sunday.

There it sat in its red foil and netted glory—all 8 to 10
pounds of it—along with a giant cantaloupe, a cherry pie and a
half gallon of Breyers' best.

The kin were coming and I aimed to prove to my relatives
that despite months of preterm labor and complications, despite one semidry pot roast, a turkey or two cooked with innards, I was a woman who could be counted on to lay out an
Easter spread with all the trimmings. It was the least I could
offer considering all they do for me, which is dinner nearly
every Sunday evening.

I knew I should have called in the troops at Heavenly Ham,
but I didn't have the money for a honey-glazed, spiral-cut to
feed a dozen. Plus, my husband got in trouble for dumping our
garbage in the Heavenly Ham's trash bin. The manager called
our house and threatened to cart him off to jail.

This is why I had to haul in a Gwaltney, at least knowing
better than to carry the heavy load up the stairs to the front
door all by my enormously pregnant self.

I heaved the bags toward my then-5-year-old son. "Honey,
don't strain yourself," I said. "But if you can get this ham up
the steps, I'll give you five bucks."

His eyes twinkled at the prospect of all the candy the cash
would buy. He grabbed the groceries, looking for all the world
like a sapped burrow as he trudged step after step, finally making it inside.

The next morning's sun slipped through my Roman shades
announcing with tapping panic waves in my chest that this was
it. Easter had dawned. A child hopped on my bed and nudged
away the remaining dreams.

"Mom, did the Easter Bunny not come yet?" Eager eyes were
on me, and the bed moved with my son's hopeful little bounces.

"The who? The what didn't come?" I rubbed my ever-contracting cantankerous belly. Whatever was in there wanted out, and it felt as if my fine fetus was slowly deconstructing a stick-built house, one bone, one rib, one muscle and one tendon at a time.

"Last year he brought me two rubber snakes, a solid chocolate rabbit and Gummi Bears," my son said, brown eyes shining with advancing tears.

Oh my Lord, I'd forgotten about the Easter Bunny. What kind of sorry mother forgets the Easter Bunny for her only child living out of the womb? As a young girl, my family did Santa and the Tooth Fairy, but Mama told us from the time we could understand the word "NO," that there was no such thing as an Easter Bunny, just the Easter Jesus.

She'd buy us each a new dress and patent leather Mary Janes for church, and we'd hide eggs and eat chocolate rabbits, but the bunny's arrival on Easter morning was never celebrated. No one would steal the Lord's thunder. And not unless a divine rabbit learned to rise up from the dead would it have a place in our lives on Easter Sunday.

"Sweetie," I said to my child. "Don't you remember mom and dad got you those new Nikes and that *Edible Bugs From Around the World* book for Easter?"

"That wasn't from the Easter Bunny," he said softly, voice starting to tremble. "Will he come tonight instead?"

A giant contraction hit and I crawled back into bed, wondering where I'd failed as a mother. "He may be bringing your little sister for a present."

"That doesn't count. She was coming anyway," he said.

Soon as he said it, the mother of all labor pains knocked the breath out of me and I howled like some kind of animal baying at a full moon.

Later that morning I called a certain member of the blood kin to report signs of true labor, wondering if I'd be able to weasel out of cooking dinner. "I'm about to give birth and not sure how I can get the ham and potato—"

"Well, can I come give you a hand?" came the kind reply. "I'll be over in a little while to help you out with the meal."

Whoa! 'Scuse me. Did you hear I'm about to give birth? And here you are still thinking I'm going to get out of bed and cook your hungry hiney a ham?

"I'm really not sure I'll be able to—"

The relative protested. "Women cook and give birth every day. It's a normal cycle of events. I can't tell you the number of babies that just fell out of a woman's housedress while she stood at the sink peeling potatoes. What time shall we be there for dinner?"

I was stunned. "Well, if I'm not in the OR with my baby and me hooked to life support and fetal monitors, you can come around sixish."

"Very good. I'll bring the rolls. I found some the other day you don't have to cook or microwave. Just take them out of the bag and that's it."

In the South when a woman promises her in-laws a Sunday or holiday meal, she'd better deliver or else.

Just as I was about to get all upset, I remembered forgetting the Easter Bunny.

"Listen," I said, changing the subject, "You know that ridiculous mockery of the Lord called the Easter Bunny? You know how he's been hopping around for years trying to one-up Jesus, and in many households he's succeeded? We don't want Niles to think there's really an—"

Silence. A cough. "What does this mean? That you're taking away the magic of his childhood? What's wrong with the notion of a rabbit coming and bringing treats and goodies? My children grew up with the Easter Bunny coming and it didn't affect our religion."

How could I say, *"Your son is agnostic. Probably the result of believing a giant pellet-pooping bunny was his salvation in the form of Cadbury Eggs and pastel M&Ms?"*

That's just it. You don't say it. You suck it up and apologize for being a crappy mother who thinks only of herself and the baby half-wedged between the cavernous womb and birth.

"I forgot about the bunny because I've been so worried about having a healthy baby," I said. "But you know, instead of all that rabbit nonsense, I read Niles stories about the resurrection of Christ and told him this was the true meaning of Easter."

"That's about as bad as forgetting Santa Claus," my kin said, laughing ever-so-sweetly and passive-aggressively. "Don't worry. I've bought plenty of extra candy, figuring something like this might happen. You just tell him the Easter Bunny isn't stiff and dead and came here by mistake."

Bless her sweet ham-starved heart. A woman that generous surely deserves an Easter spread, I thought, and immediately dialed my mother's number as I felt the baby's leg enter the birth canal. Or maybe it was an intestine or my imagination or something even more sinister.

"Mama, help me. I'm in premature labor and can't seem to worm my way out of this dinner." I cried and threw a conniption and the hormones poured from tear ducts and other orifices.

"Well, who in their right mind wants to cook?" my rational mother asked. "Nobody ever really wants to do the cooking, but you have to be gracious."

"How can I be gracious when something's trying to exit my hoo-hoo?"

"You can just shove it back up there. It's probably just your bladder. Tons of us have been tucking bladders back in for years. It's a family trait. You're bound to get it."

"What? Are you saying my—"

"I'm saying all sorts of pressure is in the womb and pushing down, and things just up and fall out of the vagina. It could be anything. A piece of esophagus, a lung lobe, an extra yard or two of intestine. Unless it's crying and resembles a skull, just shove it all back up there 'til the time comes."

"I forgot the Easter Bunny, too, Mom. I'm the town's worst mother. I'll bet even the strippers down at Joe's Titty Shack got their kids stuff from the Easter Bunny."

"Calm down. Get a hold of yourself. Jesus is all that child needs."

"Mama?"

"What?" She sounded thoroughly annoyed.

"Something just fell out of me."

"Did what?"

"The plug?"

"The what?"

"I've lost my plug."

"What plug? I've been a woman nearly sixty years and never heard of anything called a plug."

"It's the pink membrane thing that holds in the baby."

She was not impressed. "Back when my generation was having babies, there was NO such thing as plugs, uteruses, syndromes, Kegels, constant fetal monitoring and all this crazy worrying. You got pregnant, you carried on and cooked and mothered and did everything you usually did until it was time for the doctor to say spread 'em and the gas man to knock you out with whatever it was they used so we didn't have to see and hear everything going on down there."

Thirty minutes after Mama's pep talk, I was in the kitchen making pasta salad, chopping broccoli and cherry tomatoes and getting blown up by a can of room-temperature biscuits. My uterus felt as if it would drop like the ball in Times Square, and I cursed every person on earth who decided hulks of ham should be the centerpiece for this holiday instead of feather-weight tea cakes or even fish sticks. I could do some frozen fish sticks, sisters. It's one of the kitchen virgin's specialties. This traditional and formal 30-pound dinner, however, had to go on.

Around 6 PM the guests began arriving as I stooped and hauled the Gwaltney out of the oven, grabbing my tightening belly, praying to get through this night without spilling things

from my Victoria's Secret Whopper Woman underpants. I un-
wrapped the red foil and to my utter horror, discovered I'd
cooked the meat in the plastic bag along with other doodads
meant to be thrown out before heating.

Casting an eye around the room, I found no one looking
before stooping again to rescue the cherry pie, feeling hot
black plastic run down my oven mitt. Oh, no, no, no. I'd also
cooked the pie in its plastic container.

Determined, I sliced through the plastic, trying to hack it
out of the meat, yet secretly hoping someone would get a piece
caught in his or her teeth. A girl can get pretty mean during a
contraction, and I was suffering them every ten minutes.

"Hmmm. Smells delicious," a relative said, not a bit bothered that I was now lying down on the kitchen floor and panting. "You really shouldn't have gone to all the trouble." This
was the general consensus once the food was cooked, the table
set and the guests had cast their eyes on the pregnant woman
clutching her organs. It's not their fault, God love them. No
one should be forced to do the biggest meals of the year for
the rest of their lives, and it was my time—pregnant or otherwise—to lay out the spread.

After dinner, during which I managed to remain semi-
upright albeit tilted to the right, Southern hospitality drained
to zero. I excused myself to lie down and read *What to Expect
When You're Expecting*, a truly frightening chunk of prenatal
literature designed to send the fragile hypochondriacs into
great shock with such gems as, "Never eat undercooked pork,"
or the baby might have two heads, and "NEVER try to get out
of bed during preterm labor," lest you want a baby in the
Neonatal Intensive Care Unit for up to four months.

I slammed the book in a drawer and called my mother, having given her time to get home and digest the plastic remnants
from the Gwaltney.

"Mother, pack your bags, I'm having a baby, possibly by morning, if not in the next hour."

"What? How do you know? Is that what the doctor said?"

"No, I don't need a doctor to tell me when something's trying to crawl out of my body. I have all the signs. Listen, get ready just in case. And by the way . . ."

"Yes?"

"I'm changing the baby's name if she comes in the next forty-eight hours."

"To what now, honey?"

"Gwaltney. Gwaltney Reinhardt."

For those not with child or those with child firmly secured in utero, here is one of Katy Caire's recipes for Easter ham. Katy wasn't on a budget and preferred the fine hams from Kentucky, which she says are the most delicious and memorable.

Easter Ham

Katy says if you aren't going for the best hams, then concentrate on the special glazes and basting sauces to "do you proud," and lift your offering out of the ordinary run-of-the-mill category. While she varies her glazes and sauces, she prefers to blend prepared mustard with brown sugar or molasses into a smooth paste. She also scores the ham and studs it with whole cloves before popping it into the oven on Bake 300 (for precooked hams).

"Then from time to time," she wrote, "I give it a generous drink of orange juice or Coca-Cola, beer or Burgundy wine, according to my mood and what I find on the shelves." The timetable, she said, of course varies with the size of the ham, whether it's precooked or just needs "beautifying." Take a slice off every now and then for a taste to see how things are going.

For the accompanying sauce, dribble more of the basting liquid if needed, or add a dash of Worcestershire or hot pepper sauce. Serve with pickled peaches and sweet potatoes baked in their jackets, lavished with butter, and throw in an assortment of green vegetables for the perfect meal.

One of the most delicious recipes I've ever had is my mother's marinated carrots, which I call Pennies from Heaven. I hate carrots, yet I could consume this entire batch in a couple of days. It's the perfect side dish to an Easter meal—or any meal, for that matter.

Pennies From Heaven
(Marinated carrots)

Best to marinate this overnight.

2-pound bunch of carrots
1 medium onion
1 green pepper
1 can tomato soup
¾ cup white vinegar
1 tsp. dry mustard
1 tsp. Worcestershire sauce
1 tsp. black pepper
½ cup salad oil
1 cup sugar

Slice carrots till your arm falls off. Cook until tender and done. Drain well.

Dice onions when your arm feels better or have someone help you.

Also, dice the green pepper.

All this chopping and dicing will pay off. People hate to bite into half-assed chopping.

Add the other ingredients and pour over the carrots.

Marinate and chill overnight.

Serve in the marinade (don't drain).

CHAPTER SIX
Bon Appe-Cheat!

(How 'bout my own cooking show?)

If anyone's listening, I want to be on a cooking show. I realize there are plenty of men and women, harried and married, hardworking and plumb tired, who drive like magnetized ants straight for the 99-cent Value Menu every night. What they need to break this unhealthy mold is to watch someone on one of the food channels offering easy meals in ten minutes or less.

I'm that woman.

We have no role models except the great chefs who are either beautiful, outrageously skilled or both. We, however, are in the camp that thaws out a frozen dinner, tosses in a carrot or two plus a Flintstones Multivitamin, and figures the kids are good to go and cancer proofed, especially if we pour them that glass of lifesaving Florida orange juice.

My show, if anyone cares, and I'm sure very few do, is to be called *Cheatin' and Eatin'* or *Bon Appe-Cheat!* and is made up entirely of original and simple dinners along with recipes so easy a chimp could cook them.

We vow to check our pretension at the door as soon as cameras roll on the set of *Cheatin' and Eatin'*. We will be as down-to-earth as the vegetables we use.

Those showy TV cooks—who wow the crowds with condiments and exotic ingredients, portions not big enough to feed gerbils and generally speared with a giantess green onion or similarly rising sprout—are not for us.

These fancy chefs may try for witticisms and score big, wielding their knives and high-dollar wines so that I'm afraid to eat the 732 ingredients embedded in their Trout-à-la-every-thing on earth.

I'm just begging for a fifteen-minute spot on *Bon Appe-Cheat* and here's what we'd feature: a trio of chefs.

Me in an apron made of shrunken Spandex, a garment that would also serve as a body girdle, though no one would be at all aware due to the giant crab claws snapping up and down the fabric and accentuating key body parts.

Chef Number 2 would be a fabulous gay black man with wonderful clothes and hair, who would flip his soft hands and say in a girlish drawl things like, "There's nothing in this world wrong with the Hamburger Helper's Stroganoff line. With the right topping, it's to die for."

Chef Number 3 would be the puffy frumpster trucked in just to make me look skinnier and smarter. She would fry SPAM with onions and be on hand to prepare most of the desserts, such as Sara Lee's cheesecake. "Make it your own," she'd say, "by adding another layer of whip cream and perhaps some crunched-up HEATH bars."

My role would be to joke around and throw out a bunch of one-liners, even relationship advice. "Yes, sister kitchen virgins, it's true. Men don't really know if it comes in a box or can. They just want in your britches. I'm here to tell you if they clean up the dishes, then give them fifteen minutes of your finest china. Make that Va-china! Ha!" I envision letters pouring in, people wanting to know what to cook in order to get their husbands to perform or boyfriends to commit.

"Darlings," I'd say in my perfected Scarlet O'Hara accent. "There's no way to be guaranteed a diamond engagement ring simply from serving meals. Men aren't that easy. You have to threaten them. Tell them about how rat poisoning has been linked with the best hot wings this side of El Paso, and ask him whether he'd like blue cheese or ranch dressing with his."

After the advice, I'd demonstrate two to three quick and easy dinners.

"Tonight, treat your family to Tuna Tune-up, and watch the love spread across their faces," I might say into the camera, and then smile before cranking up the can opener and freeing Chicken of the Sea.

Starkist Needs a Tune-Up

Here's a superquick dinner for those nights when you'd rather curl up under the bed and scream for everyone to mosey down the road and hit another house up for eats.

Take a bunch of cans (say, three) of yummy white albacore tuna and drain. *It's better chilled.*

Mix with lots of lemon juice and pepper and Duke's mayo. *Is there any other kind?*

Toss in a few shakes of balsamic vinegar and a can of chickpeas, halved cherry tomatoes and shredded (not grated) Parmesan cheese.

I realize it sounds yucky, but it's really a tuna treat. The chickpeas are the trick. That and the vinegar and Duke's mayo.

P.S. Don't try to sub with cheap tuna. The kids will see the black skinlet things that look gross and won't even try a bite, so spend 25 cents more for the good stuff.

Dip So Divine

Mix a can of black beans, a cup or so of sharp cheddar cheese and heat.

Add salsa—as much or as little, as hot or as mild as you prefer.

Pour a couple Dos Equis or plain old sweet teas and ring that dinner bell with pride.

If you have kids, fill their greedy hands with some Tostito's.

Salmon That Almost Killed My Dog

This is pretty delicious by my standards, but has been known to nearly put canine diners in enough pancreatic distress to deem them critically ill, not to mention your bank account once the gut-blowing bill arrives.

Warning given, here you go.

Place fresh salmon (fillets or steaks) in a pan.

Take a fork and stab them (*good stress reliever*) prior to drizzling in lemon and melted butter.

Top this off with garlic and KEN'S Fat Free Raspberry Pecan Dressing and, of course, grill or bake it.

Then see if everyone at your table doesn't fall utterly and madly in love with you.

If not, send them along to the ER.

Best Beef Stew Ever

Buy a package of stew beef or whatever kind of meat you like and can afford.

In a large pan, cook meat in loads of balsamic vinegar and a spoon or two of olive oil.

In another pot, pour in a can of cream of celery soup, a can of cream of mushroom soup, ½ cup or more of Merlot, a giant can of Veg-All, a 15-ounce can of crushed tomatoes, 1 cup of water and seasonings of choice. When meat is done, dump everything into the big pot of stew. *Enjoy.*

Eatin' and Cheatin' foods, also known as Bon Appe-Cheat recipes, are all originals and not to be stolen. Only those wishing to offer prize money may copy and pretend to have invented these concoctions. The food is tested around midnight in the private kitchens of a couple of chefs, including this one, the gay black man's and frumpy lady's.

Salmon Swiss Melt

You really can't get too much salmon. Everyone claims it's the fountain of dewy-skinned youth.

Buy one regular size can of Chicken of the Sea boneless pink salmon.

Use a ½ 15-ounce can of peas (crowder, black-eyed . . . whatever), a dollop of Creamy Cucumber Salad Dressing and balsamic vinegar *(which can make a rubber boot taste good).*

Combine and spread over toast with a slice of Swiss. Pop in the toaster oven until golden brown and the cheese has melted. *Yum.*

Chef Boyardee Rocks

1 can Chef Boyardee Ravioli (cheese or beef)
1 cup cooked broccoli florets
1 cup or more of cheddar or mozzarella cheese

Open can and pour ravioli in a tiny and adorable baking dish. Add cooked broccoli and layer with cheese. Microwave.

Tuna Helper on Life Support

A box of Tuna Helper, the Fettucinni Alfredo kind, cooked as directed.

Add steamed broccoli or asparagus cuts *(for zest, culture and class)*.

Add lots of mozzarella. When finished, top with crushed potato chips *(for that blue-collar, I'm-not-above-this crunch)*.

Not long after I presented these recipes and the idea of having my own cooking show with tons of shortcuts to pre-boxed, frozen and canned foods, others have come out of the culinary closet with their prized quickies for edible, if not aesthetically appealing meals.

Remember, anything beats a meal that's all one color. That is the top mistake to avoid and I did it again the other night. I fixed spaghetti with homemade meatballs, served it with a ruby-red marinara sauce and luscious red cherry pie for dessert. Dang. Naturally, the pie was a Mrs. Smith's, because it's my belief that if something, ANYTHING, on the plate is homemade, the rest can be from boxes, bags and packets.

The "Frumpy Chef" also wanted to add her quick and delicious, "classier" cheatin' recipes, so I allowed it since I do get to feel skinnier while standing next to her.

Cucumber Salad

Slice up 2 peeled cucumbers.

Add 1 small onion. Make sure it's all sliced very thin. *(Chunky onions make a cook look slack and lazy.)*

Pour in about a ½ cup of cider vinegar and a little oil, maybe a ¼ cup.

If you want it fancy, add fresh dill.

Fruit Salad

Take a bunch of berries and some cut-up melon, apples, peaches, whatever.

Put it all into a bowl and add vanilla yogurt as a dressing.

Want it fancy? Add fresh mint.

My favorite easy, cheatin' recipe from the Frumpy Chef is . . .

Pasta and Greens

"This one is healthy, too," she said.

Sauté up some greens.

(Notice the word "up," which in the South is serious business. You UP and marry. You UP and die. You UP and sauté greens.)

Use any kind you want. *(No need to shave them.)*

Place minced garlic in olive oil in a large bowl. Add some cooked pasta and pour on a little balsamic vinegar. Sprinkle on *(we love the word "on," too)*, some grated Parmesan cheese and if you want to perk it up, add toasted pine nuts.

Serve with Italian bread.

CHAPTER SEVEN

Dude Food

Young men setting out on their own remind me of baby birds kicked out of the nest. Many plunge to the grown world in a clueless clump of flying feathers. This is particularly true when it comes to feeding themselves.

They are, for the most part, so used to Mama Bird gathering, swallowing and regurgitating supper for them that cooking a meal themselves is a much greater feat than agreeing to get neutered. 'Scuse me, make that vasectomyized.

Many of these poor creatures have invented their own system of cooking (and existing), and I like to call what some manage to swallow and digest "Dude Food."

It's not pretty, y'all, and can range from strange to downright disgusting. If Nacho Normal Nachos and Tuffie Sandwiches (recipes follow) don't get the saliva flowing and mastication gears grinding, try my friend Randy T. Ford's two selections. The former Chippendale dancer turned exotic bird therapist has suffered many a night at the GE range in complete distress. It was a lot easier when women threw dollars at him and would bake anything Betty Crocker boxed.

Soon as His Hine Ass hung up his G-string, the meals disappeared as well. Thank goodness for what these survivalist men have in common, which is an ability to make edible the grossest concoction of ingredients, hence the name Dude Food.

In honor of a friend whose longtime bride bolted and took the *Joy of Cooking* with her, I'm devoting this segment of Dude Food to the single males who find themselves eyeing their stovetops the way a toddler might stare at the *New York Times* crossword puzzle.

Leave it to a guy to come up with some of the craziest and nastiest-sounding recipes known to exist. Such is with my aforementioned, newly single friend. He had company coming for dinner and did his best to whip up an appetizing home-cooked meal. Here's what he served.

Nacho Normal Nachos

Take a big old bag of Nacho Cheese Doritos, a package of Swiss cheese and some picante sauce.

Lay the Doritos on an oven-proof plate and smother them in slices of Swiss. Pour on the picante and heat on 300 degrees in microwave till done.

I asked my friend why he didn't use regular corn chips like other people. "They get soggy," he said. "The Doritos stay chippier."

Duh. Why didn't we gals think of that? He was so pleased with himself he offered another recipe.

Tuffie Sandwiches

Run to the store and get a big loaf of Italian bread and slice it into three Hoagie-style sandwiches.

Layer with all kinds of manly cold cuts *(the kind that gives a person horrible breath)*.

Don't forget to add pepperoni and top with Swiss cheese.

Put each sandwich in a plastic bag and stick it in the microwave for two minutes *(or just until the bag explodes)*.

"The bread gets all moist and chewy," Doritos Man said. *"My kids love them because they're so tough. It's great when we're trying to pull teeth or make a little extra cash from the Tooth Fairy."*

I asked him why not nuke a Goodyear tire instead of the bread, but he said that wasn't funny so I let the matter drop.

I'm sorry, gals, but few women, unless drunk or five days into the show *Survivor* (forced televised starvation), would touch most of this stuff.

Dude Delight Omelet

Cut up some hot dogs or veggie dogs and throw them in a pan with eggs and butter and tons of cheese.

To jazz it up, toss in vegetables. Place a sprig of parsley on the plate.

Dude Chow

Select one of your favorite flavors of Ramen noodles. Add a bunch of veggies.

Add water and microwave for enough minutes to cook it all.

Top with soy sauce and voilà! *A meal fit for a single dude and with enough salt to entice cattle.*

Here's a Dude Food recipe from my very own husband, TIDY STU, who, while in college, clung to his roommates at dinnertime since all were challenged when it came to finding meals. Stuart took a shine to making omelets, which seem a healthy staple among college boys. When he decided the cheese and eggs were making him fat, he switched to Recipe Number Two.

See, the thing is, men will eat one or two dishes all year long. They don't seem to need variety anywhere but the bedroom. Ever noticed?

Here is his waist-reducing recipe that costs less than $1.50 for the entire meal and takes two minutes to prepare.

Tuna and Trees

Open up a can of white albacore chunk tuna in water. Plop it on a plate.

"Cut you off a few broccoli florets and there you have it," he says. *"A fine meal."*
I'm thinking, "Where's the Duke's mayo? The relish? The celery? The pickle juice? The chopped Vidalia onion?"

Dudes only care about feeling full and pay little attention, especially when they're clueless college kids, about the divine ingredients that could take a meal from suck to succulent.

Other times, Tidy and friends would rush to Pork Chop Night at the Roman Room in Knoxville, where he was at the University of Tennessee majoring in music. "We couldn't wait till Pork Chop Night," he said. "It gave us something to look forward to all week long."

I'll never forget the first meal he ever made for me. We'd been dating about two weeks and he asked me to his early-nineteenth-century log cabin for dinner. The cabin, from the outside, looked exactly like something the Beverly Hillbillies would claim, but inside it shone like a little gem.

A rather strong, though not offensive aroma of fish and rice seemed to butter the air as I sat and waited for the feast to begin.

He proudly served my plate, which, colorwise, earned an A-plus. The fish was whitish, the rice wild and multihued, and the broccoli shone a vibrant green, which few Southerners strive for. Typically broccoli at the hands of true Southern cooks isn't "ready" until it's almost a brownish-green and the consistency of mush.

Fairly quickly into the meal, I noticed something wasn't

right about the fish. It appeared to have a thick silver-black band around it, as if it was wearing a scuba suit.

I picked the scuba skin with a fork, afraid but smiling with good manners and carefully controlled grimaces. I ate the rice, which was nice and cooked to perfection. I speared some broccoli—good, but in need of at least one seasoning. Water and broccoli was all he used. No butter, no salt. Still . . . edible.

"Don't you like fish?" he asked, digging into his Scuba Fillet.

"Oh, I love it. Smells great." I watched him eat more, but was still not sure how to secretly dispose of the fish without him knowing I didn't eat a bite.

As kids, Sandy and I were experts at clandestinely trashing food while eating Thanksgiving at our great-grandmother's house. Believe it or not, little kids generally hate turkey and dressing (especially dressing, which as adults most of us cannot seem to get enough of). So we always scooped it in a napkin, then pretended to need to use the sink to wash something off our hands, where we'd dispose of the dressing in the garbage. Great-grandmother none the wiser.

Stuart's eyes bore a hole in me that evening of his debut meal, and I had no choice but to take a bite of that strange fish. I put my fork in the center, far from the rubberized edges and produced a small bite. I chewed. And chewed. And chewed. It wasn't bad-tasting, but the texture was one that I couldn't digest.

"Hmm. What is this?" I asked, swallowing the rest whole to avoid more chewing.

"It's shark," he said with pride. "In many countries it's a delicacy."

Well, not in this one, I wanted to say. In this country, it's cheap fish. Poor man. He really had tried so I managed to eat about one-third of the shark, but when he excused himself to pour more tea, I pulled the Thanksgiving stunt and wrapped the rest in a napkin and dropped it in the garbage can.

You gotta give a guy an A for effort. Plenty of them will try, especially if they think it will score points leading to the Sealy and Serta extrafirms.

College boys and young adult males who are lost souls at the stove tend to find buffets and other cheap eats where they can fill up and not have to worry about another meal that day. It was at one of these very places I ran into a friend who boasted of his heritage and culinary prowess.

"I'm half-German and half-Jew," he said, and patted his rounded stomach.

We began talking about Dude Food and he lit up like a Christmas rooftop when asked for his favorite recipes.

My first mistake was asking for his cherished foods while my stomach was bloated from having consumed too much sushi and Diet Coke. Sushi, which will be addressed more fully later, is a taste Southerners must acquire, and having only recently acquired it, I was afraid it was about to repeat on me.

Especially upon hearing him describe his signature dish.

Darin's Death of Romance Irish Gruel

"It's not nasty," he promised, still all lit up and happy. "I'll invite you over, and you'll want to marry me for how good it tastes."

He said his first wife left him for his lack of cooking skills so he's in the market for a new wife.

Without further ado, here is his stew.

First, make some lumpy Irish oatmeal.

"I'm not sure," he said, "what the lumps are, but they're good. I sing a song when I make it that goes, 'I'm going to eat those lumps, I am. I'm going to eat those lumps, yes ma'am.' "

Cook the oatmeal the long way. Don't use instant.

When it is just lumpy enough, pour in some beans. Any kind will do.

"I like Boston Baked Beans. They're so cute they look like little cockroaches in the gruel."

Heat it all up. Pour it in a bowl and enjoy.

"It will be a creamy beige color, and you won't be able to tell if you have a lump or a bean when eating it."

"It's so very filling," Darin said. "That's the most important and only requirement for Dude Food is that it be filling. But it's wonderful, too. It's serious food. The amount of gas you get from this could start a small natural power plant if you hooked it up to your BVDs or a pipe organ."

When Darin isn't making his gruel or hitting up the buffets, he does what many men (and women) do. He eats cereal.

"It's just as good for lunch and dinner as it is for breakfast."

His second and final recipe sounds only a tad better than the gruel. For those with steel stomachs here you go.

Darin's German Peanut Divine

Take two pieces of Jewish Rye Bread and spread one with lumpy cashew butter.

"It's like peanut butter," he said, "only more expensive and organic."

Put raspberry jelly on it—excessively. Top with other slice.

Drop it in a little hot oil in a pan to make the bread nice and crunchy.

"This one is really delicious," Darin promises.
By the way, he's still single, God love him.

CHAPTER EIGHT

Upscale Dude Food

Allen Boyd, 49, has been cooking since age 13 when his mom started taking classes to better her education instead of her copper pot collection.

"After my second or third TV dinner, I decided if I wanted to eat well, I'd better learn to cook," this strapping 6'8" sequoia of a fellow said.

"The first TV dinner is kind of neat, a novelty," he said. "The second OK, and by the third, it's getting really old."

"As you may recall," he continued, "I used to spend the weekends in the kitchen with Dad, learning the one-hand egg break and how to make good Southern breakfast foods like grits and liver mush and country ham and redeye gravy."

Boyd hasn't faced a kitchen yet that didn't present him opportunities to create his favorite dishes. Here are but a few. You have to marry him to get the rest. Seriously.

"It's my recipe, and I'm allowed to do a little cheating," he said.

Big Al's Bad-Ass Wings

Buy a bunch of chicken wings.
Get a bottle of Texas Pete Chicken Wing Sauce.

Use ½ bottle of KRAFT Honey Barbecue Sauce.
Chop up a habanero pepper.

Put it all in a pan and let it simmer while cooking the
hot wings.

Put hot wings in olive oil, and cook just to the point
where a fork will go in and slip out easily. *You don't want
to overcook your chicken.*

Take chicken and put it in a pan of sauce and turn it
over and over until good and thick.

*"Then I make my own blue-cheese dressing," he said. "I do
it to taste."*

Take Roquefort blue cheese, a little mayo, some buttermilk and minced garlic. Mix together and that's Al's
dressing.

*"Everybody's that's ever had them loved them," Al says of his
hot wings and dressing. "They're a lot better than the wings at
Hooter's."*

*As for heat, Al said his recipe is "stupid hot. Past a Category 10,"
he warns. "If it weren't for the blue-cheese dressing, you'd be blistered
from one end to another. It's also good for worming. If anything is
living in your intestinal tract, it'll be dead."*

Big Al's Redneck Spaghetti

*"Rednecks are just a little bit lazy," admits Allen, who purely
loves being a Southern, government-hating male. "We have many
activities and it's hard to find time to cook a big meal."*

"So we get us a jar of Ragú *(Super Chunky Mushroom is
his favorite).* And instead of ground beef, I get a pound of
Jimmy Dean Country Sausage, and I fry up my sausage.

"Then I cut me up half a white onion to add sweetness, take me two heaping tablespoons of garlic out of a jar, enough to kill a vampire and keep skeeters away."

He says there's not a lot of grease to pour off the Jimmy Dean as with the cheaper sausages.

"After you get everything simmering good and the onions nice and soft, I grab that big jar of Ragú and pour it in there and put it on low while I get my pasta—regular old spaghetti—ready. Pour a splash of olive oil in the pasta."

Because Allen is nearly 7 feet tall, the meal makes two servings. For normal-height people, it will feed six.

"*It's delicious,*" he said. "*Once I did it this way, I can't go back to the ground beef, which tastes boring now.*"

Another man who boasts a degree in culinary arts and can dance his way around a kitchen as if it were a ballroom floor is my friend Mark Bennett.

I met him years ago during an outdoor festival when I'd bought one of those suspicious meat-on-a-stick things, thinking it was tender chicken, and handed it to my preschool daughter. She took a bite and almost immediately began choking, thus I began to scream and do the Heimlich maneuver on her, while everyone thought I was a child abuser, except Mark, who came to the rescue.

"That could not of been chicken," I said, panting and relieved my daughter coughed up the meat and was OK. It must have been a donkey haunch. In fact, most of the meat there was more than likely slabs of old T. rex, wolverine or donkey haunches.

Mark and I got to talking, and he said he was a chef with an associate's degree in culinary science.

If I'd have had dentures, they'd have fallen to the asphalt and done a *clickety-clack* dance. He didn't really look the "type" who could cook, whatever that type is. He was skinny as a Whippet.

"I've wanted to cook since I was two," he told me one day after I ran into him at a local restaurant. "In high school French class we learned how to make cheese fondue."

He needs to meet Walt Mussell, the Food Channel addict and aspiring author of *Honey, You're Annoying Me! 49 Spouse-Irritating Habits That Women Know and Men Need to Find Out.* He's also a chef by his own right who says he takes recipes from the network and from various cookbooks and "makes them my own." Kind of sounds like Randy Jackson, one of the *American Idol* judges who's always telling contestants, "Yo, dude, you took that song and you made it your own."

Here are Walt's finest and favorite Upscale Dude Food recipes. Mark was supposed to send his but didn't. He is missing in action.

The All-Purpose Stir-Fry

The All-Purpose Stir-Fry recipe was something Walt "developed" (for lack of a better word) during his bachelor days. After cooking a number of dishes from a Chinese cookbook, he eventually realized that what he was doing could be synthesized into one all-purpose recipe for creating a multitude of dishes.

"Following this recipe, most anyone should be able to prepare stir-fry meals simply and quickly," he said. "However, it should be realized that none of what can be created from the steps below should ever be mistaken for real Chinese food. If you want real Chinese food, your choices are as follows: 1) be born into a Chinese family, 2) marry into a Chinese family, or 3) discover which Chinese restaurant in your area attracts local Chinese nationals and begin frequenting it."

Walt says that when planning to stir-fry, you should always check the fridge, freezer and pantry to see if you already have any of the ingredients needed, as there are so many.

"At my house, we usually have frozen chicken in the freezer, some vegetables in the fridge and various canned items in the pantry (bamboo shoots, pineapple, etc.). Cleaning out what's in the house can sometimes give you a better feeling than going to the grocery store and buying whatever you want to cook."

Meat/Seafood (choose one): a) chicken, b) pork, c) beef, d) shrimp, e) scallops. Estimate the amount needed at ½ pound per adult person eating. Defrost prior to cooking.

Veggie/Fruit (choose as many as desired): a) carrots, b) mushrooms, c) broccoli, d) snow peas, e) bell pepper (any color), f) pineapple

Optional: onions

Spice (choose at least one): a) ginger, b) cumin, c) Chinese five-spice, d) chili pepper, e) paprika. (*Actually, there are any number of spices that one can choose. It's up to personal taste.*)

Other Optional (choose one): a) bamboo shoots, b) water chestnuts

Oil (choose one): a) cooking oil, b) extra-virgin olive oil

Optional Oil/Liquid (choose one, if desired): a) sesame oil, b) fire oil, c) some other one

You will also need 1 or 2 cloves of garlic, soy sauce, cornstarch and water.

Step 1: Wash your hands.

Step 2: If choosing chicken, pork or beef, either: a) Cut into small single-bite pieces or b) Cut into large single-bite pieces.

(*Note: Shrimp and scallops should already be the proper size.*) *If choosing shrimp, make sure it is peeled and deveined. Place the bite-size items into a bowl.*

Step 3: Wash your hands again. *(Remember, you were dealing with raw meat.)*

Step 4: Pour oil choice and a little soy sauce into a bowl, coating your Meat/Seafood choice. Add Spice choice. Add optional oil choice, if desired. Cover and refrigerate to marinate.

Step 5: Using a different cutting board and knife than those you used in Step 2, chop/slice/dice your Veggie/Fruit choice and set aside. Slice/dice/crush garlic clove(s) and set aside. If you also want onions, chop/slice/dice them and set aside.

Step 6: Place large saucepan on stove at medium heat. Add two tablespoons of your oil choice and allow to get hot. Once heated, add garlic to pan and cook for 1 minute. Remove marinated Meat/Seafood from fridge and add to pan, along with a bit of the marinade. Stir and cook until pieces are browned and cooked through (about 3–6 minutes). Remove Meat/Seafood from pan and set aside.

Step 7: Add a dash of oil to pan. Add onions, if desired, and cook for 1 minute, stirring periodically. Add Veggie/Fruit choice and cook for 1–2 minutes, stirring periodically. Add optional oil/liquid choice, if desired, and cook for an additional minute.

Step 8: Return Meat/Seafood choice to pan, stirring occasionally.

Step 9: Mix about a teaspoon of cornstarch in a small amount of water, making sure that no cornstarch lumps exist. Pour starch-water mix into the pan. Allow to simmer. This will turn your marinade into something of a thickened sauce.

Step 10: When sauce has thickened, turn off the heat and serve your dinner.

Step 11: After dinner, clean up. Make sure that any kitchen counter surface that was touched by raw meat/

seafood is cleaned and disinfected. Ensure that any cutting boards used are washed in the dishwasher or are washed with soap and hot water.

Post-recipe comment: "This recipe wasn't the only concoction I made during my bachelor days. However, it is one of only two that I remember and the only one that I still make today, even after eleven-plus years of marriage."

Walt's Masala Chicken

This recipe arose from Walt's first foray with the South Beach Diet. For those of you not familiar with the diet, the first two weeks of it are called Phase I. During Phase I, dieters alter their style of eating, abstaining from such foods as fruits and pastas. After the first two weeks, you start adding them back (in Phases II and III).

Though the diet book provides many recipes for Phase I, Walt grew frustrated with the limitations and started developing new recipes daily during the second week.

"My wife tried every dish that I made," he said of his lucky bride. "Of all the dishes I created that second week, the one below is the only one that she commented she would actually eat again."

Best if marinated overnight.

2 or 3 6-oz. chicken breasts
2 Tbsp. garam masala
2 Tbsp. powdered ginger
2 Tbsp. soy sauce
2 Tbsp. extra-virgin olive oil
Splash of sesame oil
Step 1: Place chicken breasts into a bowl. Add soy sauce, extra-virgin olive oil and sesame oil, making sure to coat the chicken well. Sprinkle the ginger and garam

masala onto the chicken, making sure to coat both sides.

Step 2: Cover the bowl and place into the fridge. Marinate for at least 30 minutes and, if possible, overnight.

Step 3: Preheat broiler. Line broiler pan with aluminum foil. Place chicken on foil. Broil on Low Broil for 20 minutes.

Step 4: Remove from oven and serve.

Walt lost 12 pounds the first two weeks on the diet. I, personally, fainted after being on South Beach for three hours.

As for the superscrumptious dishes featured from Walt, I'm not sure the average kitchen virgin could pull them off, however, I plan to at least try one of them. The tough part is finding all those mysterious spices. Whatever happened to "a dash of salt, a teaspoon of pepper?"

One more male who's an extraordinary cook is "Drive-by Dave" Presley of Missouri. He has a lot to say about everything, food notwithstanding.

One of his prized recipes is Dave's Cashew Chicken.

"WARNING!" he shouts. "This is not a health meal. It took me years to perfect my recipe, but my friends think it's better than the restaurants."

When I saw the list of ingredients involved, I knew I'd NEVER attempt to prepare such greatness. My favorite cookbook is called *Four Ingredients or Less.* My favorite phrase is "take-out."

But Drive-by Dave is tenacious in his cooking exploits. A regular on a Branson, Missouri, radio station, Drive-by Dave is all humor and clownish capers. He enjoys preparing Oriental dishes while cranking up tunes such as "Turning Japanese," by the Vapors.

"I also have a little bottle of sake to make the cooking go easier," he said. Proving my theory that people who like to cook tend to enjoy drinking along with it. Makes it less of a chore.

Drive-by Dave's Cashew Chicken

3 big, boneless chicken breasts with rib meat
Flour
4 Tbsp. black pepper
2 Tbsp. garlic powder
3 cans of cheap 14-ounce chicken broth (NOT FAT-FREE!)
4 Tbsp. oyster sauce
2 Tbsp. Mirin
1 Tbsp. teriyaki sauce (optional)
3 or 4 large eggs
Buttermilk
Vegetable oil (enough for a deep fryer)
Egg rolls
Pot stickers
Dried hot mustard
Cornstarch
Rice
Green tea
Green onions, chopped
Cashew pieces

"The first thing you do is pour yourself a big old glass of sake," Dave said.

Cut the breasts into small pieces. Cut off rib pieces and put to the side.

Get out a big freezer bag and fill it with a ¼ cup of flour.

Add pepper and garlic powder. Shake well.

Pour another glass of sake.

Now, get out a medium to large saucepan and add 2½

cans of the cheap chicken broth. Save other ½ can for later.

Put in the saved rib fat, oyster sauce, Mirin and teriyaki sauce.

Cook over medium heat for now, while stirring.

Get out a big glass bowl and crack eggs into it, and add the buttermilk. Whisk until a thick, yellow consistency.

Pour another glass of sake.

In a deep fryer, heat vegetable oil to 375 degrees.

Check on your sauce. You need to boil it for a couple of minutes to dissolve some of that rib fat, then turn to a simmer.

Take several pieces of chicken and submerge them into the eggs and buttermilk mixture.

One at a time, pull the chicken pieces out, put them into the bag of flour mix and shake like there is no tomorrow.

Go ahead and fry your egg rolls and pot stickers and put them in the oven on WARM.

Get a beer.

By now you are burned out on the sake and you need to start getting it together for the guests.

One at a time, drop the chicken into the oil. *(One mistake most dudes make is trying to put in too much chicken at one time.)*

The chicken needs to be crispy, yet not overcooked. You will be frying several batches, so put them in the oven with egg rolls on WARM.

Cook the rice.

Make the hot mustard sauce by mixing two teaspoons of mustard powder with two teaspoons of water. You might need to triple this.

Add cornstarch to the sauce, turn up the heat, grab another beer and stir the sauce. If too thick, add leftover chicken broth until you are happy with it.

Serve the chicken in a big Oriental bowl.

Replay "Turning Japanese" *song.*

Sprinkle the cashews and chopped green onions over chicken.

Serve the rice, egg rolls and pot stickers on the side.

Let the guests decide if they want to pour the sauce on the chicken or use it for dipping along with the mustard sauce.

Serves four to six.

"Me and my friends think this recipe kicks ass," Drive-by Dave said.

Since this was written, Drive-by Dave has purchased a Cruzin Cooler and motors about the streets of Springfield, Missouri, atop the giant cooler filled with beer and powered by 500 watts.

It's a step below a moped. God love him.

I warned him that the law would pop him for a DUI whether riding a giant goat, a canoe or a cooler. He seems happy, though, pink-cheeked and cruzin' at 12 to 14 mph with a buzz on.

He wanted me to include the recipe for his pickled eggs, an original dish that he made up one night after too many trips to the cooler. When he said the fumes of this dish caused him to see his grandmother who'd been dead thirty-five years, I figured I best leave it out.

God, I love Drive-by Dave.

CHAPTER NINE

Monster Collards and Daisy Shavers

Believe it or not, there's a town in North Carolina that has an annual collards festival. For more than thirty years Ayden has celebrated collards, believing that by hosting such a festival the town could bring new people and vitality into the area.

Lawmakers in Raleigh, North Carolina, voted to designate Ayden as the site of the first such festival deeming it "The Official Collard Festival of the State of North Carolina." Apparently, when a town gets the government behind a fruit or vegetable, big money rolls in and people want to move to the area. The town even has a logo that says, "Peace, Love & Collard Greens."

It's nice to see collards are finally getting the recognition they deserve.

One can't have Thanksgiving in the South without serving greens of some kind, preferably collards. It was a cooking act I falsely believed couldn't be all that hard.

I mean, what we are talking about here is a bunch of leaves, right? I envisioned cooking spinach and how simple it is to boil the things, the ease with which they shrivel up to nothing.

Therefore, when faced with yet another Thanksgiving meal to host, I bought two messes of collards and some bacon, and decided to be a true Southern cook. Only I went about this collard business all wrong.

I rinsed two clusters, the leaves long as snakes, in the sink. Then I boiled water and stuffed them in. When they turned a beautiful light green, I figured they were done. Kind of like broccoli. No one wants dirt-brown broccoli. We want vibrant florets, unless you're true Southern-to-the-artery-clogged core and then the browner the vegetable, the better.

As I prepared the collards, I failed to cut off most of the stems and spines, figuring they were all part of the fine-dining experience. Such assumptions are big mistakes many a kitchen virgin suffers.

The meal, once I pulled off all the kinfolks' eyewear and plied everyone with enough wine, would be spectacular, I thought. I had no idea that when it was all over, they would talk behind my back about each and every dish served.

"Susan's collards were longer than my forearm," Mama told Aunt Essie about six hours postdigestion. "Bless her heart. It was like pulling a big eel out of a lagoon. One of mine even had a mouth like a carp. I picked that thing up and it kept going and going. First time I ever needed a knife to cut my collards."

I asked Daddy what he thought, and being a true Southern gentleman loyal to his daughters, he was merciful and forgiving.

"They weren't the best collards in the world, but I enjoyed mine," he said. "They were different. I could pick up the stem and eat the leaf that was shaped kind of like one of those big ol' handheld church fans."

'Tis a tragedy if a middle-aged woman can't even make a mess of collards, so I decided to get with the program and ask for suggestions and recipes.

I no longer wanted to serve collards tough as horse saddles and long as water snakes. I asked a friend who's a Yankee how to cook them and was surprised at her vast collarding knowledge. She advised "deveining" them along with a thorough slicing and washing.

My daddy says some people put collards in the washing machine on the gentle cycle to get rid of the bitter juices they produce.

"Your grandmama would wash them in the bathtub and put two great big old pots on the stove. She'd cook them down to nothing, then take them out and wash them again. She'd start out with what looked like an entire field of greens and end up with just a quart or two.

"You can't believe how many collards it takes when you cook them all the way to done. The key word being *done*."

The message being mine weren't done. He was kind about that, too.

"I'm sorry about my collards, Daddy," I said for the tenth time.

"It's OK, hon. I just chewed right through the spine and considered it my daily roughage intake."

When I wrote a column for the paper about my failure to produce decent collards, my friend Pamela Carman had a story to beat them all. She's a hoot of a woman who always has her nose to news and an ear for the eccentric, and lives on the outskirts of Asheville in a remote area tucked in the very western corner of the state.

I love this woman and her sassy daughter, Hansi, who was both a firefighter and Mrs. Plus Size North Carolina. It wasn't long after I ran the piece about my carplike collards that Pam received a phone call from her precious Hansi.

"Did you read Susan Reinhardt's column about the collards?" Hansi asked.

"Susan who? I don't read the newspaper."

"Liar. So you did see it. I guess you know what it reminded me of." Hansi couldn't catch her breath she was laughing so hard at the visions of her mother's past collarding efforts. Pamela knew exactly what was coming.

"I suppose you have called," she said, "to remind me of the time I shaved the collards. Don't you think that's wearing a little thin?"

The story will never wear thin in this family. It was during the "farm phase" of marriage number three that Pam's husband suggested she might ought to pick a mess of collards for supper.

"Collards were new to me," Pam said. "Now, I had seen cooked collards, tasted them and was not favorably impressed. I ranked them one notch above boiled okra, a substance that always conjures up memories of sick babies and little blue-nose aspirators."

She decided to go ahead and do her wifely collard duty and set about digging in the dirt for a mess, which she dumped into the sink and got the shock of her life. They were covered in tiny hairs.

"Hairy collards!" she squawked. *What was this stuff that had emerged from her fine earth?*

As she began washing them, her arms sprouted a bunch of hives everywhere the collards touched her skin. "Surely you can't eat these hairs." She didn't recall seeing hair on her kinfolk's collards and wondered what she could possibly do to remedy the situation.

Well, what would Lucille Ball do?

Pamela Carman took her sharpest razor, no doubt a pink Daisy quadruple-blade, and decided to shave each leaf as if it were a human leg. Her family has never let her live it down, especially Hansi, who keeps insisting her mother must have been confusing collards with mustard greens or some other leafy vegetation.

"I'll bet you don't know collard greens from mustard greens from spinach," Hansi said.

"Well, who cares anyway? They're all the same," Pam snapped.

"No way. You ever heard of collard quiche? That sounds just like something you'd try and cook up."

Not to be outdone, Pam had something to hold over her

own daughter's head, and quite literally so. She begged Hansi for a truce.

"If you lay off the old collard-shaving story, I won't bring up the bird thing again."

"Bird thing?"

"I promise to never again tell anybody about the time you put Aunt Sally's parrot on your head and he got his feet all tangled in your hair and I had to put a pillowcase over your head to keep him quiet while I drove you to the vet's office to get him untangled."

The image of her daughter in the backseat, pillowcase jumping and twitching as the cars passed and passengers stared aghast, is one she'll never forget.

"And I still recall what you looked like when the vet lifted the pillowcase," Pam said. "Your hair was full of feathers and bird poop. He treated us both like we were lunatics."

For those lunatics who truly want to know how to cook a mess of North Carolina collards, check out *www.chitterlings. com*. I visited and learned a whole lot about these greens. The webmaster Willie Crawford wrote *Soul Food Recipes*, and provided his family secrets for Awesome Collard Greens. It is not for vegetarians or those who like healthy living.

Awesome Collard Greens

2 or 3 smoked ham hocks or smoked neck bones.
5 pounds collards (several large bunches)

Add some salt to a large pot of water and crank it up to a boil. Throw in the meat for about 1½ hours. *(You'll want the meat falling off the bone before adding the collards.)*

Collards: Rinse each leaf individually in cold water. To cut: stack several leaves, then roll them together and slice into thin strips.

Add collards to the pot. Cook on medium for 30 minutes (or until desired tenderness).

"People in my neck of the woods," says Crawford, *"usually sprinkle lots of hot sauce on their collards. Give it a try."*

Hazel Hollifield has another recipe for collards:

Easy Collards with Hog Jowls

Take two bunches of fresh collard greens. Cut them into bite-size pieces. *(Don't forget to remove the tough part of the greens.)* Season.
Simmer till Grandma can chew with her false teeth.

Buy a few pounds of fat hog jowls.
Fry until all the grease comes out and the meat is crisp and tender. Save the grease.

When the collards become tender, pour the "pot liquor" off (this would be the liquid in the pot), and let the collards cool.
Then pour the hog jowl grease on the collards in a frying pan. Simmer (actually, fry) for another hour.
Put in a little "Salt of the Earth," to suit the taste.

"This menu is supposed to bring you the best of everything, such as good luck, wealth, happiness and I don't recall what all," Hollifield said. *"Some of it seems to have worked for me. And if all that grease don't make us have plugged-up arteries, we all might make it until the next New Year's dinner."*

CHAPTER TEN

Tricks and Bad Eats

No grown woman gets more excited about going trick-or-treating than I do. It's the one and only holiday when nobody expects a cooked meal. In fact, it's just the opposite.

Grown-ups and kids alike force down bits of a slapped-together sandwich or a piece of fruit before charging into the night to collect the loot. Some mothers have even been known to give their kids a Red Bull so as to keep them moving from house to house more quickly, filling up those king-size pillowcases with everything Hershey ever made.

Being completely addicted to chocolate, I was the kid who, back in the seventies, went trick-or-treating for two consecutive nights, nearly causing Mama to have a heart attack to go along with a string of hissy fits. It's not proper for children who were raised right to trick-or-treat on the wrong day—or Heaven forbid!—two days running.

Sister Sandy and I had spent a chilly Halloween night going from street to street, neighborhoods laid out neatly, like rows of corn. For some reason, greed got the best of us, and the next night we slipped out after dinner and knocked on doors, ringing bells.

"Trick-or-treat!" we yelled at the wide-eyed and confused.

"Why, I thought Halloween was last night," astonished residents said.

"I know, but we were sick." We coughed and feigned weak voices. "I had a 106 fever and Sandy threw up part of her prostate." (We had no idea where the prostate was located, and since they didn't do sex ed in elementary school back then, we didn't know it was a man organ.) "If she doesn't get candy she'll be scarred for life," I said, pointing to my younger sister who was all but suffocating in her paper Cinderella mask. "Her prostate is gone and we'll probably have to get on the organ donor list."

Of course, they didn't want to ruin a child's life and so fished in their leftovers to produce enough candy. When our parents found out, I'm quite certain we were grounded, spanked and stripped of our allowance for several weeks, that being an era of more corporal parental control over children. Everybody in those days got whipped, and no one's mama was carted off to the Department of Social Services. I'm not saying this is a good thing. I'm just reporting the facts.

Halloween had always been a big deal for my sister and me who grew up in a small Georgia town just a few miles from the Alabama line. We celebrated the holiday first with a trip to the Great Pumpkin Patch, located on the Piggly Wiggly sidewalk, followed by the Saturday-morning gutting of our selection.

With bare hands, we yanked out the stringy pulp, seeds and juices, releasing the smell of fall as it ran in sticky streams down our forearms. We sliced and jabbed until a face appeared, one looking more aghast than haunted.

My mother wasn't like the other moms who enjoyed sewing Broadway-caliber costumes for their tots and bragging to everyone, "I made that antebellum Scarlet O'Hara dress in just short of three days. Isn't it adorable?"

Mama claimed only one thing made her meaner than cooking and that was sewing, which would consume her, clouding her religious convictions, making her forget Proverbs and glide toward cussfests.

Instead of pumping her Singer and threading bobbins, she took us to a dime store, where we had the yearly thrill of choosing a paper-thin costume that, I swear, if you licked it, would disintegrate right on your tongue.

We knew which houses gave good candy. And we knew which houses passed out the cheap stuff. For years we mapped out our roads to sugar highs and would stay out for hours.

One question some have during Halloween is, "How old is too old for trick-or-treating?" In most towns, it is accepted that kids participate at least into adolescence. In our town—more forgiving of individual quirks—trick-or-treating stretched beyond the normal cycle.

My sister and I trick-or-treated throughout our late teens, though my mother refused to buy any more costumes.

"You're on your own," she said when I turned 17 and reached for the king-size pillowcase. "I want no part in this embarrassment. Hide your face and don't tell anybody you're my child."

After high school graduation, there would be no more trick-or-treating for the many barren years that lay ahead. Then, when I got pregnant with my first child, a lightbulb went off. "Remember how much fun we used to have on Halloween?" I asked my sister, who nodded and licked her top lip in anticipation.

"Well, guess what? I'm pregnant, which means we can go trick-or-treating this year. I'll be far enough along that it will be obvious to everyone, and when they ask who I'm getting candy for, I'll just point to my tummy."

She convinced me this wasn't natural and could earn jail time, so I agreed to wait a year, and the following Halloween, in 1993, I dressed my infant son like a lion and off we went, door to door, my baby in his stroller, my hand holding a loot bag.

My sister, a few months pregnant, joined in the fun, put on a costume and came along with us for old-time's sake. She, too, carried a tub for collecting.

Those answering the door seemed aghast.

"Be careful the little one doesn't choke," a lady said as she doled out the candy. "I'd give you some Gerber, but we don't have any. I hope to the dear Lord you're seeing a specialist." Tsk. Tsk.

"Oh, don't worry," I assured her, knowing the chocolates would never mix with Gerber, and knowing my sister and I would polish off the candy in two days. "We'll save a lot of this until the baby's top teeth come in. If we're lucky enough to get some TEEF!"

As our children grew older, they realized their mothers were SERIOUS trick-or-treaters and they'd have to guard their pumpkins and loot bags from the get-go.

Thinking about all of this, I realized that if someone asked what were the top two reasons for giving birth, I'd say: 1. To fulfill a personal or biological need to reproduce and experience infinite love. And 2. Having kids is a way to go trick-or-treating for many more years than the nonbreeding population can do so.

On the other side of Halloween night, the side not related to eating and collecting candy, are those who love to give out the goods—or in some cases, the sour pickles, and the ketchup and other condiments. These days, you never know what will land in the loot bag.

A friend of mine got a pack of Camels one year. Another friend, J.D., who is an artist and pronounces his name something like Jaeeeedeee, gives the most bizarre Halloween booty of anyone I personally know.

Forget apples and raisins. Those look great compared to what Jaeeeedeee sneaks in their bags and plastic pumpkins.

"What do you give them?" I asked, and he smirked and then sort of grinned.

"I give them condoms," is what I thought he said. But he is

so soft-spoken, you have to slap his chest a few times to rustle certain words to the surface.

"You give what? Did you just say you give them—"

"CONDIMENTS!" he said louder.

I thought about this. Hmmm. I wonder which item might be worse. Condoms or condiments?

"You mean you give out salt and pepper?" I asked. Lawsy. I'd never heard the word condiment till I worked one summer at Wendy's when we had to ask salivating customers, "Would you care for condiments with that single cheese, sir?" Where I grew up, we just called them "packets of stuff."

"What do they say when you give them condiments?"

Jaeeeedeee shifted from foot to foot. "They don't know till later. I don't hold them out on a display tray. I curl up my hand so they don't see what I'm putting in there."

Well, mercy, I guess not. I can see it now. You got your Horsy Sauce from Arby's (my personal favorite), Hunt's ketchup, Gulden's mustard, soy and duck sauces from the various Chinese joints, and the mother lode from Taco Bell (mild, moderate, hot, fire and "boil me alive" sauces).

I asked Jaeeedeee if he ever got yelled at or had his house egged. He said the kids usually don't discover his gifts till he's shut and locked his door.

"I find them on the driveway the next day," he said of the condiments. "Most of the kids have thrown them out and stomped on them."

"I can see their point."

"It's healthier," he said.

"Yes, I'd imagine so."

"If they come to my house, they have to take what I give them."

That's the rule. Come and get it, kiddos. Mmmmmm. I hope I get some tarter sauce this year or a few packs of Splenda.

If you think Jaeeeedeee is bad, you haven't been to my sister's on Halloween night.

"We're giving out decorated plastic bags filled with an assortment of gherkins," she said from her minimansion in Rich City, Georgia, where money grows on trees and people drive golf carts.

I wasn't sure I'd heard correctly. Cell phones not only distort sound but can also, according to Mama, destroy the brain and cause infertility, or worse, a rabidlike personality. Where she gets this I have no clue.

"Gherkins?" I asked. "Aren't those pickles?"

"Best you can buy. Only top-of-the-line for Rich City, Gawgia, trick-or-treaters."

She's got it all planned what she is going to spring upon the costumed hopefuls and is preparing to say.

"Look at you, precious Snow White. Why I bet you could use a bag of sweet gherkin chips."

"Oh, and look at little Darth Vader. Hmm. He's definitely a dill."

I asked dear Sister Sandy what would be the point of a gherkin Halloween instead of one sponsored by Hershey.

"Oh, the looks on those faces will be priceless," she said. "Just like they've bit into radishes. We plan to videotape it all, but are also going to give them real candy, too. We aren't that mean."

"What if you run out of pickles?" I asked.

"No problem. One of the Daves (the name of her two husbands, past and present) will just slice up some fresh squash."

"SQUASH?"

After this first act of my sister's Halloween fun is over, they've hatched another in the wings, she said, a mean giggle rising up from her throat.

Chad, Sandy's 12-year-old, plans to put on a full scarecrow suit and sit on the front porch as still as the dead. He will hold in his hands a bowl of yummy candies with a sign that says, PLEASE, ONLY ONE. WE MUST SHARE WITH OTHERS.

And if a paw snatches up more than the allotted request? "He'll scream at all those who try to take more," Sandy said. "A bloodcurdling scream. He may even slap them."

I asked my sis if she didn't think her Halloween plans were a bit on the weirdo side, even for us.

"Yes, of course they are, but either way, they get gherkins and real candy. It's a win-win. Just think what their parents will say when Belle from *Beauty And The Beast* shows them her little bags of pickles.

"It's good old-fashioned fun. I'm tired of everyone leaving the trick out of trick-or-treating. This is a big part of it and no one gets hurt."

I gave it some thought and wondered how I could spruce up my own Halloween that year, only to come home from work on a Friday to find my daughter in a blissful mood and hot-pink wig.

"What's this get-up you got on?" I asked. "You look like a ballerina after a round of bong hits."

"What's a bong?" asked her little friend Anna Herbert from London and fairly new to this Southern town.

"It's . . . it's . . . well . . . that noise a drum makes," I said.

"We're not ballerinas," my daughter said. "We're dancing divarinas. We wore these to go trick-or-treating after school today."

"Today. TODAY?"

I checked my head and found the battery half-dead. I checked my cell phone calendar and found it was fully charged.

"Girls, there are eighteen more days until Halloween, the official night when people dress up and can legally extort neighbors for candy."

They fished about for a piece of chocolate, and on closer inspection, I felt stunned. This was not a bite-size Butterfinger. This was a Belgian truffle, a $2 or $3 confection.

"Where did you get this?" I asked, impressed by the candy's quality and the costumes the girls had worn.

"Mrs. Parham gave us each a piece to tote on home," Anna said, her British accent tainted with Southern expressions. (I was relieved Miss Anna didn't say, *"She done give us each a piece,"* or her parents might ban her from our home.)

I called Margie Parham who lives across the street to confirm the preholiday sugar grubbers.

"They came to the door and said, 'Trick-or-treat, dancing feet, give me something good to eat.' And I said, 'Hold on a minute. Let me see if I have any candy.' I didn't have much, but I had a bowl of my expensive personal stash."

Thank goodness she used to be a schoolteacher and was laughing.

"I told them to tell their mothers 'hello,' " she said. And I loved her for not adding, *"Why the heck would any decent mother allow her child to tart up like that and mosey out two and a half weeks ahead of schedule?"*

"It was good fun," Margie said of the girls' activity. "They thanked me and everything. They didn't come over here doing anything ugly, it was just to have a good time and get candy on top of it. I consider that pretty smart. It's October and they wanted some candy."

I called Anna's parents to let them know the girls had pulled one over on the cul-de-sac and had loot bags to prove it.

"I think their early start is simply a by-product of what they do in stores in America's consumerist culture," said Anna's father, Stephen Herbert, his British accent unmarred by Southernese. "I saw a Christmas tree in one of the big department stores yesterday, therefore, the kids are sent the message it's easy to go out and do things early."

Maybe he has a good point. I'd rather my chirrins haul out the costumes and plastic pumpkins and fish for candy in early October than whip up a meth lab or sit in front of the TV all day.

Here are other good reasons it's not a bad idea to buck up and trick-or-treat early.

1. You'll get more candy. Especially the yummy kind you weren't supposed to have.

2. You might get money, particularly from those who have no candy and are caught red-faced and empty-handed.

3. The kids will get lots of mileage out of those expensive and poorly made costumes. Think four rounds of trick-or-treating versus one.

4. Any neighbors one might secretly wish to hiss at can be dealt with by sending over a gaggle of chocolate-starved Gothic ballerinas.

5. Parents will benefit by having extra time to either check the candy for worms and lead paint or eat it themselves.

HALLOWEEN

Halloween Treats

Buy bags of real chocolate candy like TWIX Cookie Bars, M&Ms, Snickers, Butterfingers, etc.

Remember, kids don't like hard candy, though pricewise, it's beneficial for the buyer.

For more fun on this night of ghouls and goblins, give out weird things such as radishes or pickles, but always follow them with a piece or two of good candy.

Easy and Healthful Meal
—Pump Something in Them—
Prior to Trick-or-Treating

Your choice of peanut butter
Whole wheat bread *(if your kids will go for it)*
Jelly of choice
Half an apple or other fruit
Milk

CHAPTER ELEVEN

When Roadkill Meets Mikasa

Mama Dot protected and memorialized roadkill.

Aunt Betty opened up her mink coat and invited it home for supper.

They say when you put a woman in a mink coat and a Mercedes 450 SL, she'll begin to act the part.

She'll become a queenly thing, batting her eyes hither and yon, speaking softly and waving with barely a twist of the ulna and radial bones.

I'd say that might sum up most women in high-dollar coats and cars.

'Course they never met Aunt Betty. But you have. At least readers who've been around awhile and have read my books or columns know about my wild Aunt Betty and her crazy-lady ways. They know she once gave blood while all liquored up from a Bloody Mary lunch at the Red Lobster. They know she passed out on the table and got sick and Mama had to hose her down in the backyard like livestock.

They know she cuts splits and cartwheels, is over 70 years old and continues scheduling doctors to tack up her innards when they fall below sea level in her body. But nothing stops her.

Aunt Betty is a kitchen virgin by choice. She knows how to

cook but hates it, leaving the task to her second husband, whose specialty is barbecuing butts.

She also enjoys dressing to the nines and dashing about town in her little gold Mercedes.

Not long ago my Uncle John bought her a full-length mink coat after she'd hinted for years. She was in heaven with that soft fur touching her bare skin. Now, don't go getting in a snit. She loves animals and takes exceptional care of her pets but has not crossed the line into PETA territory. A fur coat, in her mind, was perfectly PC to accept and wear with pride.

The occasion to actually wear the coat was another story. Finally, the day presented itself when my cousin went into labor and gave birth to a baby girl.

The weather was frigid in Spartanburg, South Carolina, where Aunt Betty lives and where ice storms do more than their fair share of damage.

She ignored the threats of slick roads and potential death, fixed up her face as if going to a ball and slid into the leather seats of her sweet little ride.

She arrived at the hospital to see her ex-husband all aglow with his new bride, and she was pleased as punch she'd decided to go all out and wear the mink and fancy leather gloves.

"It was gorgeous," she said breathlessly of her coat. "I mean gorgeous."

Once in the hospital room, she congratulated her daughter and peered at the dark-haired, olive-skinned baby girl.

"She looked just like a little Indian princess," said my aunt who has always claimed Cherokee blood. "She was absolutely beautiful."

After oohing and ahhing over her new granddaughter, Aunt B. asked her big, tall son-in-law to please walk her to the car. It was dark and the ice had begun settling on the roads.

"I got bundled up in my beautiful coat and fine leather gloves and was about to get in the elevator when an orderly stopped me."

"That coat must feel good on an evening like this," he said, stroking the soft fur as my aunt all but purred. She stepped into the elevator with her handsome and very young son-in-law.

"There were two very fine matronly looking ladies in there and I saw them admiring the coat and snuggled my head up under Mark's arm all cozy and cuddly."

The ladies stared at the floor-length coat. "Ohhhh," one of them said. "Your coat is magnificent."

Aunt Betty batted her eyes and scooted in closer to her son-in-law. "Thank you." Then she did what she does best. She shocked them. "You know, not only is my fellow handsome and young, he's also rich."

The ladies said nothing else and quickly got off the elevator.

On the way home, Aunt Betty wondered what in the world she and John would have for dinner. She did not feel like cooking unless mixing a Dirty Martini counted.

As she thought about the day's events, she heard a thud underneath her car. She slowed and felt her heart jump in her throat.

"I thought, 'Oh, my God, I've run over something.' I got out and looked and it was a little bunny laying under my back tire looking just like it was asleep. I cried and said a prayer and then I picked it up by its feet and put him in the back of my Mercedes, grinning all the way home."

She got out of the car, rabbit in her gloved clutches.

"John," she said. "Here's our dinner. "Clean him and cook it."

Two hours later they ate fried rabbit, biscuits, and rice and gravy. "Remains and Rice," I called it.

The next day my cousins heard tale of this and had a fit.

"My kids laugh about Mama driving in her mink coat and fancy leather gloves and fine Mercedes, picking up roadkill," Aunt B. said.

Aunt Betty isn't the only one eating Remains and Rice for supper. Remember Hansi Holloway? The one who got a parrot caught in her hair and whose mother shaved the collards?

This Mrs. North Carolina Plus America, a former firefighter and mother of three, hosted a foreign exchange student in her youth.

This is the same woman who growing up admitted her mother couldn't cook diddly squat, and when she was coming along, had to fend for herself or starve. Hansi, as we've learned, comes from a colorful family. That's the genteel word we in the South use for "bona-fide insane." "Verifiable" is another word we throw out to explain and excuse those who are "tetched in the haid," more correctly written as "touched in the head."

Sounds so much better than "crazy," doesn't it?

Being a girl who claims she had to learn to cook on her own, Hansi said that her mother once married a man who expected his wife to operate a range.

"I came home one night all excited because I was told we were having cornbread," Hansi said. "Used to be, I had to go next door to get cornbread and biscuits. I was about 12 or 13. When they finally hollered for us to come eat supper, I came running down the stairs and took one look at the cornbread and knew I was in trouble. It had molded to the shape of the plate and looked like a Frisbee. It was so tough we couldn't cut it and looked like a concrete birdbath."

Hansi didn't want to hurt her mother's feelings.

"We ripped a piece off and slapped some butter on it," she said. "I tried to bite into it and actually broke a bunch of brackets holding my braces together. It was kind of like the papier-mâché I had in kindergarten."

Hansi is like me—she can't cook all that well. "The first time I ever made supper," she said, "I was engaged and had moved to Orlando on my own. I had my own apartment, and set it up and decorated it so cute. I'd just turned 18 and was so excited and proud of myself, I thought I owned the world."

What she didn't own were stove-top skills. "I decided to have my fiancé and my little brother over for supper, and went to the store and bought me some chicken. I was going to make fried chicken, fresh tomatoes, and homemade creamed corn and biscuits.

"I didn't figure it would be hard . . . no big deal."

Hansi prepared the dinner, cooking her little heart out. She set the table, had the candles glowing and giving off pleasant yet not overbearing scents, and checked on her dinner. Everything seemed fine, almost glorious, even.

"The chicken was the most beautiful light-golden brown, the biscuits came out perfect—white and fluffy—my first attempt and I was so proud of myself."

Hansi recalled everyone eagerly sitting down for supper. "The first thing I did was bite into the biscuits, which I was particularly looking forward to since Mama can't cook them. Doug tried the corn. My little brother Stephen bit into the chicken. When he did, he looked like a vampire and blood ran down both sides of his mouth.

"How long did you cook this chicken?" he asked.

"Oh, about five minutes," Hansi said.

She hasn't cooked another chicken to this day, poor woman.

I always buy mine already roasted at the grocery store for $4.99. Often, truth be told, they are as close to raw as legally permitted, but what do you expect for supper under five bucks? To solve the problem, nuke the bird for 10 minutes and it's good to go.

Hansi said her cooking feats pale in comparison to the time her sister, who was in boarding school, brought her boyfriend, a poor young man from Denmark, home one weekend. "My ex-husband, being the big hunter he was, had found out Nicoli had never been hunting," Hansi said.

"You ain't never been huntin', huh?" Hansi's ex-Bubba-hubby asked.

Nicoli was cute, blond and blue-eyed. About the only thing they hunt in Denmark is other blue-eyed people.

"My ex smears hunting paint on him and gets Nicoli up at the crack of dawn to hunt squirrels," Hansi said. "He'd forced the boy to go along with him, but Nicoli came home so proud of himself. He'd killed one squirrel."

"You gone have to scunt that squirrel," her ex told the poor, delicate Denmarkite.

"Scunt," Nicoli said, oh-so-cutely with that little accent that makes you want to squeeze a boy hard as you can.

"You got to peel off the whole hide," ex-Bubba-hubby said. "You gotta bare-ass that sucker if you gonna cook him."

Nicoli's face registered alarm and then quick recovery.

This innocent and first-time squirrel killer obliged, wanting to fit in with the culture of this country he was visiting.

"When he brought it in," Hansi said of the squirrel, "it looked like a naked Chihuahua with testicles."

Nicoli partook of the squirrel meat without getting sick.

"He hurried back to Copenhagen earlier than scheduled, and we haven't heard from him since," Hansi reported.

OTHER ROADKILL TIDBITS

This just in from Joyce Dover, a woman who admits the occasional cooking weakness.

"Shortly after I was married, my grandmother told my husband that she would like for him to catch a possum and bring it to her," Dover said. "In her younger days, my grandmother's mother would cook possum so my grandmother, apparently, had cultivated a taste for this ugly rodent."

Dover said her husband nabbed one as it was sneaking around the back door of their home. "He had trapped it in a sack (I don't know how because you couldn't have pushed me anywhere near where the action was going on), and we took the smelly thing to my grandmother."

The woman lit up like a ball field, purely elated she had a possum to cook.

"Thing is, my grandmother was a clean woman and she would never cook that oversized rat until she kept it for a couple of weeks," Dover explained. "She put it under a big tin tub on her back porch and she began to feed it clean, wholesome foods to fatten it up. Maw believed that you could clean a possum by feeding it and holding it hostage so it couldn't eat trash and other roadkills."

Within that first week, Maw gave that possum more than it could eat. One evening she went to feed it, and when she lifted the edge of the tin tub, the fat possum waddled out so fast no one could have caught it.

"She had been looking forward to roast possum and told us that we could come eat with her," Dover said. "I would never have touched that rodent, much less taken a bite of it."

My great-grandmother and namesake also loved roasted possum. Publicly announcing your kin eats roadkill is putting yourself into a giant Southern redneck stereotype.

My great-grandmother (also named Mama Dot) could have afforded regular meat, such as chicken and pot roast, but she and her husband, Papa Dot, had a penchant for possum.

My late great-grandfather, a man I remember wearing little round glasses, having a permanent tobacco stain in the crease of his chin, and smoking a deeply curved pipe from his red leather chair, was purely crazy over cooked possum.

It was my mother who revealed the family's dark secret.

"Please, Mama," I begged. "You're kidding, right?"

"Oh, no. He'd go out just before sunrise and hunt them for his stews. He wanted to find them early, before they stiffened up."

"What do you mean, 'before they stiffened up?'" I asked, hoping she wasn't heading in the direction I realized she was definitely going.

"We had always thought Papa Dot went 'hunting' with a gun for his possum," Mama said, lying on the sofa late one night watching *The Guiding Light* on cable. "But you know what? Your Aunt Betty told me he was looking for fresh roadkill."

Never again will I think of that side of the family with the same regard.

I called my elegant and sophisticated Great-Aunt Rubye, hoping she'd set the record straight.

"Did Papa Dot really eat possums?" I knew she'd tell the truth, no folklore for this Cadillac-driving, world-traveling 88-year-old.

She took her sweet time answering.

"Papa Dot was an expert squirrel hunter," she said, and I breathed a sigh of relief. In my mind a squirrel was somehow higher up the food chain than a possum. But Aunt Rubye didn't leave it at that. No, she had to continue, her thoughts rewinding to the twenties and thirties when Papa Dot was a big man with a gruff voice and surly nature.

"Come to think of it, he did enjoy possum hunting," she said, and I froze. "He'd go at night and—"

"Did he get them off the roads?" I asked, interrupting. "You know, already dead?"

"You mean roadkill?" she asked. "Not that I'm aware. I believe he kept them in cages to fatten them up, like the witch did with Hansel and Gretel. Mama Dot would cook them but wouldn't serve them at the dining room table. She made him eat his possum in the kitchen, away from the rest of the family."

One morning Papa Dot went out to his cages to feed his sly-grinning meals-to-be. He lost his temper when he saw the cage doors wide-open, not a single possum scratching or hissing about.

Papa Dot's boys had gone out early and set them free.

"He was furious," Aunt Rubye said. "He never got over it."

If Papa Dot had lived in Nashville in 1999, he wouldn't have had to bother with cages and the pranks of mischievous boys.

A bill passed in which "wild animals accidentally killed by a motor vehicle may be possessed by any person for personal use and consumption."

In other words, it would be perfectly legal to make a meal off flattened fauna.

Bon Appétit, Papa Dot.

And may the golden roads of Heaven be paved with the occasional possum.

Uncle John's Scrumptious Fried Rabbit

(Otherwise known as remains and rice)

Take 1 freshly run-over rabbit.
Shake off all the fleas.
Skin it. Gut it.
Wash it.
Prepare for cooking as if it were a chicken (cut into sections).
Salt and pepper it good.
Marinate it in buttermilk for an hour or two.
Flour it.
Fry it until brown on both sides.
Once it's brown, put it back in pan, add about a ½ cup of water.
Cover and simmer for about an hour to make it tender.
For a great meal, serve with rice, gravy and biscuits.

"That makes the best gravy you've ever eaten," Aunt Betty said.

Uncle John's Best Butt

Best to marinate overnight.

1 Boston Butt*
Season with a dry rub made of salt, pepper, paprika, Worcestershire and lemon juice.
Marinate in fridge overnight.

Put it on the grill or in a smoker, and while cooking (and between Bloody Marys) baste with a mixture of brown sugar, vinegar and lots of black pepper.

Cook 8–10 hours.

Remove the bone.

Chop and serve with your favorite barbecue sauce.

*Hint: If using frozen, thaw out. If you're not marinating it right away, be sure to refrigerate as soon as thawed or else recipe then becomes "John's Stinky Butt."

Sweet Aunt Essie, the other sister, always said, "John has the best ass in town."

Here are a few savory and gamy selections from Southern humorist and writer George Motz.

"I have owned or operated five restaurants and one bar in my lifetime, besides farming," he said. "And I once wrote a cookbook, my style, practical and handy.

"Here are some good recipes, but remember they are from the north woods, and you 'Rebels' may have a hard time relating to them."

Snapping Turtle Soup

Catch one medium- to large-sized snapping turtle.

Cut off head with ax. Use ax to separate top from bottom of shell.

Using sharp knife, skin out legs, neck and tail.

Cook very slowly in water for 3–4 hours (cooking too rapidly toughens the meat).

Remove meat from bones, and toss in whatever vegetables you like (*because your wife and kids—or, in my case, ex-wife—won't eat it anyhow, Motz said*).

Broiled Skunk

"Now don't go laughing," Motz said. *"I'm part Native American and this animal is a delicacy among my people. Also, during hard times, even the whites ate it. Here is my favorite skunk recipe."*

Catch one skunk, two skunks if more than two people are to eat.

Skin, clean and remove insides.

Parboil for 15–20 minutes in heavily salted water.

Pour off water, add fresh and bring back to a boil.

Remove skunk(s). Rub on butter, salt, pepper and lemon juice.

Broil for 40 minutes, basting every 5–10 minutes in lemon juice. *(Oh, yes, remove the scent glands. Don't want to make that mistake—again!)*

If you think roadkill is gross, how about those freaky peeps eating placentas? If you are one of them, I'm sorry and am certain you have good reasons for eating human innards. Here's the story of what happens . . .

WHEN BODY PARTS BECOME DINNER

Time has marched across my face with hawks' talons. Like most women over 40, I am instantly pepped up by the notion of nonsurgical ways to look ten years younger, ten pounds lighter, ten days just back from Canyon Ranch.

I'm the proud owner of more potions and lotions than the Mistress of Makeup at a fancy department store. Sadly and expensively, most of the promises of youth and renewed beauty go unfulfilled and I wake up each morning with pillow creases and other ravages of loose-skin syndrome that take the entire day to iron themselves out.

Oh, I'll glance in the mirror on Day Two of using a product and falsely believe the eye bags have packed up and left town,

and the jowls have climbed back into firm and fighting position snugly against the mandibles. But by Day Four, the sight
is blight.

Typically, the magic ingredients that cost $100 a half ounce,
squeezed in these slender, lovely tubes and vials are of such
high quality, I end up resembling a teenager going through a
massive acne breakout. Or worse, the rich oils will seep into
my eyes as I sleep and I'll wake up looking like the sandman
poured in Crisco instead of grains of rest. I guess my bags like
cheap.

A friend was whining the other day about how old and fat
she was getting. Of course, both of us know we're not THAT
old or THAT fat, but it makes for lively conversation during
lunch breaks as we eat Tuna Melts and Lay's chips followed by
pies and cakes coworkers leave on the break room counter. We
enjoy playing the game of "Out-Fatting Each Other." Those
who leave treats instead of scarfing them are always the skinny
colleagues who eschew the Keebler elves and Godiva fairies
and secretly want us to ugly up and get porky.

"Hey," I told my friend one day as the *Oprah* e-zine flashed
across the computer screen. "You ever heard of the Age-Defying
Diet?"

"No, I have not," she said, dipping her vinegar- and chipotle-
drenched French fries in ranch dressing. "What do you have
to eat? Bean sprouts?"

According to one of Oprah's many hangers-on, Dr. Nicholas
Perricone, the weapons for fighting sags, bags and bodily jig-
gles are one sardine and anchovy away. If we follow his plan
for ten days we can wipe ten years off our faces. We will look
like Britney Spears and Lindsay Lohan postrehab. Maybe even
better. I'd eat practically anything if it promised to mimic the
genes of Angelina Jolie's face.

Hmmm. I clicked on the suggestions to see just what we'd
have to choke back to be thin and beautiful.

Perricone said we Americans lead inflammatory lifestyles
(does he mean we're prone to hemorrhoids?) that give rise to

all sorts of woes, ranging from drooping skin—what I like to call Crock-Pot flesh—to heart disease, cancer, diabetes and the other biggies. If we don't eat his gross fish choices, we'll end up looking like four-pack-a-day unfiltered Camel smokers.

What causes this, he said, and so have countless others, is sugar and anything white, processed and yummy. Yummy means ugly and deadly. Eat a Little Debbie Swiss Cake Roll and wake up looking like the decomposed. Remember that. Plus, Dr. Perricone said we don't drink enough water or eat enough dark green and colorful things. We don't get enough fiber, blah, blah, blah! Fiber people suck, and stay bolted to the toilet most of the day. They are also more prone to fart in yoga classes than are nonfiber people.

"Sugar is the No. 1 enemy," Perricone said. "It results in stiff, inflexible and sagging skin."

Stiff sounds pretty good to me. I wouldn't mind some stiff skin, since mine wiggles like a trot line of fish.

Coffee, he said (my favorite drug, the poor man's cocaine), will make you plump and ugly, too. It raises those hormones in the body that shout, "Put a layer of fat over her once-fine thighs, and give her a spare tire for having one too many creamy lattes at Starbucks."

The doctor said if you substitute green tea for coffee and do nothing else for six weeks, you can kiss ten pounds good-bye. My lips are puckering.

Here are a few other tips for beating back the clock, bush-whacking disease and dodging the ugly stick. Don't we all want to ward off the ugly stick?

Perricone advises us to down plenty of essential fatty acids necessary for elevated mood, beautiful skin and increased mental clarity. He suggests fish oil and olive oil and lots of un-salted raw nuts and seeds.

I dubbed it the "Squirrel and Rodent Diet." Even so, I'm a big sucker, and my friend and I decided to try it for five days.

"What's flax?" she asked, popping in a Milk Dud and threatening the security of her molars. "Is it a fabric like gingham? And what's this with the fatty acids? Am I going to have to pour olive oil down my gullet?"

This isn't going to be easy. We'll see who needs the Clear-asil or Haley's M-O first. In the end, we bought some sardines and gagged over our office-issued wastebaskets. We gave up and went back to vinegar fries and other white flour– and Dixie Crystal–dominated foods.

No sooner had I gotten over what Dr. Perricone recommended than did I hear about what Tom Cruise was planning to dine upon.

I didn't believe it when I read it, but supposedly Cruise told a bunch of people he was planning to feast on his beloved then-fiancée Katie Holmes's placenta after the baby was born. I can just imagine him thinking of all the possibilities: Placenta and Polenta, Placenta and Penne Pasta, Placenta Pâté. . . .

Finally, the wait was over and he and his sweet Katie gave birth to a precious baby daughter they named something weird. Well, duh. What did we expect? I guess Suri, which means princess in Hebrew and red rose in Persian, beats Bertha.

The rumor about Tom putting knife and fork to Katie's placenta is probably (hopefully) not true, but is apparently a growing trend among granola weirdoes and people who have nothing in their pantries but soy nuts. Heck, after eating years' worth of tofurkey, hummus, legumes and sprouts, a nice, fresh placenta sounds about as good as a grilled rib eye.

Kind of reminds me of Hannibal Lecter in *The Silence of the Lambs*.

When my own doctor asked if I wanted to see my baby's placenta (whose function I truly didn't fully understand) along with other by-products, I asked, "Why in the world would you think I'd want to see what's in that bucket? Is a placenta something I can use to get more baby gifts? Is it something I need to sustain this angel's life? If not, just hand me what needs to go in my cradle and toss out the rest."

"Some use it to plant trees," the doctor said.

"Do what?"

"It's so rich in nutrients. Makes trees grow twice their normal foliage."

"I'll just stick with potting soil."

Doctors have a name for this feasting on placentas—placentophagia—which is practiced in many countries and cultures.

I have a name for it, too. Fruitcakephagia. A friend of a friend who had a midwife and a water birth left her baby's placenta attached for twelve hours and then took it to the apothecary to mix up a nice concoction of vitamin tablets.

Yuck! Give me my Flintstones Chewable any day over Pro-V-Placenta.

I think Tom was jiving and going for funny when he said he might gobble up some of this stuff, but you never know with this guy. Remember, he's the one who can get pretty manic at times, yet expected his missus to luxuriate in a "silent birth." That is an oxymoron unless you are a moron.

Silent birth? Well, Mama had one, but that's only because they knocked her out cold when she started hollering up a storm and frightening all the other laboring women.

Lately, the TV and tabloids can't stop churning out the news on Tom and Katie's afterbirth and "silent birth."

For a while, people thought good old Tom meant that Katie couldn't utter a single "Get your crazy Scientology self out of my room!" while having a contraction, or wouldn't allow her to beat him about the face when at nine centimeters he's trying to feed her an ice chip or crank up a Yanni CD.

To his credit, he said if she needed a bit of medicine, she could have some. What a peach.

And to clear things up a bit, his church, that Scientology business where they probably don't even have covered-dish suppers, believes in a serene and quiet birth. It doesn't mean Katie couldn't moan a bit, maybe do some chanting, a few mantras such as "I am woman hear me roar . . . and I've been down there on the floor," by Helen Reddy.

Let's just wish them all the best. And hope someone will

bring them a covered-dish supper so poor Tom won't have to crank up the Crock-Pot, smother Suri's placenta in garlic and olive oil, and dine like Hannibal Lecter.

Surprisingly, it's not just fruitcake celebrities feasting on the birthing organ. As I said before, that friend of a friend turned her birth guts into vitamins. The other day, after having written in the newspaper about the subject, a sweet freak sent me an e-mail about the wonders of eating placentas.

"Maybe it has something to do with my wife being born and raised in northern Maine," Mr. Zamani said, "where the practice seems more acceptable (enough to be legal, at least)." Natch, this couple decided to experience the gory glory of a home birth—as in no harsh sounds, invasive medical equipment or fabulous drugs. Don't these earthies realize that the fabulous drugs are *way* worth trading in all that potential peace and quiet?

"My wife has had naturalist leanings since I've known her— never giving in to the dark side and always rejecting Western medicine or anything like that," Zamani said. "But she has a generally sensible approach to things, and this is just something that she derived from her sensibilities."

'Scuse me? Sensibilities? I guess I had no sense giving birth in a red thong, floating on Demerol with an epidural chaser?

"Living in Maine," the earth dude wrote, "and being a man who is generally unconventional, I agreed with everything, and we had a home birth and got ourselves a midwife."

Hey, dude. If midwife doesn't do epis, I have no use for her. But it's a good thing others do. Takes all kinds to make the world the strange and wonderful place it is. I applaud every single weirdo and kook. Clap, clap. Amen.

"Anyway, being an unconventional guy," he continued, "the idea of placentophagia unsurprisingly caught my attention." He admitted the absurdity of the act proved a draw, pulling intrigue from places it hibernates.

"When I was reading about this, I discovered the placenta

is the only organ ever ingested that is a result of life and not death. Plus, I just thought it was cool. A cool story to tell."

Heavens! I wouldn't eat tripe or chocolate roaches just to tell a cool story, but I'm not faulting the guy. At least he was brave. And creative.

"Participation in an assuredly harmless but GROSS gastronomical affair was bound to produce some very entertaining responses," he said.

I can hear them now. "You did what? Say you ate a what? A placenta?"

At least he cooked it. Zamani found a Placenta Roast recipe online amongst myriad other placenta dishes, proof if you Google something, you're bound to locate far more than you bargained for.

It ended up that Zamani's wife had a few complications and the couple had to forgo the home birth for a hospital delivery. After baby Asher Cain entered earth, Zamani asked the attending physician to save the placenta.

I can hear Zamani now. "Hey, buddy. Don't toss that fetus roast. I've gotta recipe for it that will feed us for a week."

The doc placed the organ in a plastic hospital bowl and Zamani slipped it in the fridge. Later in the night, a nurse came into the room and gave him the what for about storing a fresh placenta in the refrigerator.

"I learned then that the fridge had to have its contents trashed and undergo a thorough cleaning and sanitizing."

"This is not a place for medical waste," the nurse admonished. "It is a place for food."

Zamani said, "I had to bite my tongue from saying, 'Oh, but I plan on eating it.' I just let her vent and leave, and then filled the bag it was in with ice to keep Cain's placenta from spoiling."

God forbid a waste of such cannibalistically carnivorous fare.

"The next night, I was dining on Placenta Roast."

Most men would just as soon brag about eating a double order of hot wings at Hooter's. Not Zamani.

"It was a bit gamy and reminiscent of liver. My wife tried a bite but wanted no more. It wasn't that great but I ate it all except for the last few bites, which my cats wouldn't even eat when I tried to give it to them."

It was great fun, he said. "It has a romantic profundity to it."

Sorry, sweetie. Romance for me is a meal of crab legs drenched in hot melted butter.

When his daughter was born, Zamani continued his desire to honor the organ that had sustained her, but instead of cooking it, he buried the placenta beneath a young pecan tree down in Alma, Georgia.

Down in Alma, a small town leaning on the conservative side, people viewed the act as "fruity," he said. "I won't deny the oddity of my decisions."

Well, I won't deny it either. But hey, each to his or her own. I'd rather eat pig's feet or even the hooves than this stuff. For placenta recipes go to *http://www.twilightheadquarters.com/placenta.html.*

CHAPTER TWELVE

When Daddies Do the Cooking

(It's either to get toasted or laid)

Here's how my husband lays out a meal. One bag of Green Giant baby carrots, washed and peeled. One pint of fresh strawberries. Two meat patties cooked "medium cremation," or black and tough as the sole of a shoe.

When looked at from a dietician's standpoint, it's a healthy meal that meets the major food groups and doesn't topple the government's ever-changing food pyramid, save for the carcinogens of burned meat.

If my husband is feeling especially creative, he may switch the meat to chicken breasts, broiled until it appears the little birds are wearing dark leather coats. This, too, will be accompanied by baby carrots and either strawberries or blackberries. He never prepares rice, potatoes or any starch other than angel hair pasta, which takes five minutes on boil.

Again, he's laid out a decent meal and without having to cook but one of the items—the chicken or the beef. He is a smart man and understands what few of you dudes comprehend: that if he feeds the flock while I'm at work slaving, he's likely to get some affection later that evening. This is how men can get more of what they want: Turn on the range and you've turned on the woman. Heat up a chicken's breast and she'll give you her breasts.

"When I arrive home after a hard day of putting up with all the abuse I take from the public and my bosses," a working mother is wont to say, "I'd like something on the table besides the Fruity Pebbles' leftovers from breakfast."

Men learned quickly that by turning something on the stove, they have much greater chances of turning someone on the Serta.

Due to this role-changing and division of domestic duties and men taking relations wherever they can find them, we now have a rebirth of fellows in the kitchen, guys hooked on cooking shows featuring culinary hotties.

Take the case of Walt Mussell, an Atlanta-area businessman who is obsessed with cooking along with the stars of skillets, knives and garlic presses. He watches the Food Network the way some men are glued to soft-core porn channels. He grows hot about the face and "region" when a scorchingly beautiful chef comes on and turns on all six burners with the sounds of sex: hissing, sizzling, popping and banging. When it's all over, instead of multiple *O*'s, you've got multiple courses on which to feast and savor.

As for Walt, he's writing a cookbook and tests each and every recipe on his beautiful Japanese wife, who minces no words and tells him like it is.

"I have many cookbooks written by such Food Network personalities as Rachael Ray, Giada De Laurentiis, Sandra Lee and Alton Brown," Walt said. "My wife often gives me a hard time about my two favorites—Rachael and Giada—the hottest women on television."

He recalls when these two fair cooking maidens were pitted against each other during *Iron Chef America*, a Food Network show that stages cook-offs. "I felt like a preteen again watching *Charlie's Angels*," he said.

Walt, unlike most manly dudes, has piles of cookbooks, which are marked up like an old woman's Bible. He's inserted brightly colored tabs, denoting things his family enjoyed and that he'll likely prepare again.

One time his wife searched the books and left him a note telling him how much she'd appreciate his cooking a particular Giada dish.

"Adding in other recipes," he said, "I created a perfectly balanced meal. It was: Appetizer: Rachael Ray. Entrée: Giada De Laurentiis. Dessert: Sandra Lee."

Cooking wasn't always a natural for Walt, though he's been dabbling at it for twenty years—ever since his mother pushed him from the home nest and sent his hungry hiney to college.

It wasn't until he married and began arriving home earlier than his wife that he decided to become the main cook of his Georgia dwelling.

"The boys and I found ourselves waiting for Mo to come home and cook dinner," he said. "I mentioned to her that I wanted to cook, but she refused me several times."

Mercy, is this woman of sound mind? Such words would be music to my ears and fuel for future sexcapades. Here's the equation: food plus cooking equals love and Serta privileges.

Walt, also one of the few male members of the Georgia Romance Writers group, said cooking and getting some action are tricky business.

"The first time you cook something special, you'll get laid," he said. "If you cook for her again two weeks later, you'll get lucky again. The third time you cook for her, she'll have come to expect it, and it is no longer special."

If you guys want to improve the ratio, here are Walt's suggestions:

Cook for a different woman—a problem for married guys.

Cook infrequently enough so that it's not a habit.

Pay attention to what she craves as she flips through a cookbook or magazine. If she actually requests a particular dish and you agree to make it, that is nearly a binding verbal agreement, granted that women always reserve the right to change their mind.

It wasn't always so cut-and-dried for Walt. When he first

started cooking, his wife not only wasn't turned on, but was slightly horrified.

"The only thing you know how to cook is stir-fry," Mo told him as nicely as she possibly could. She feared Walt would become the typical "cooking" dad who served French fries or tater tots every night, but she was wrong, and her beloved discovered his addiction and obsession with the Food Network and can now cook anything from rice pudding to variations on the South Beach Diet dishes.

His recipes are included in the Upscale Dude Food chapter, since he's long past opening a pack of Ramen noodles and calling it a meal.

As for the majority of the men I know, the only cooking they feel comfortable doing is outdoors. The grill is the thrill, kind of like mega leaf blowers and high-powered weed whackers.

My dad is a good example. On the rare nights when he and Mama entertained at home, the food was extra special. No Mrs. Paul's Fish Sticks, none of Mama's famous Parched Dogs with the cheddar cheese tongues. These were the magical evenings when Daddy would light the grill on the patio he poured himself from wet concrete. He'd watch the grill glowing, then take a seat on the gray/blue benches he'd sawed and sanded, releasing a satisfied sigh and taking long swigs from a can of Schlitz beer. After two or three more beers, he'd grow mellow while the charcoal smells rose along with the unmistakable aroma of garlic-marinated steaks, filling the air of the warm Georgia evenings and driving my sister and me crazy with hunger.

We knew Mama was in the kitchen wrapping big Idaho potatoes in tinfoil and shoving them into the oven on Bake 350. We knew the salad tonight might have real Thousand Island from a bottle, not the ketchup-and-mayonnaise mixture. We knew if someone had given her a sweet Vidalia onion, she'd chop it up and sprinkle it on our salads, maybe even add some Bac-Os or croutons.

This is why we loved it when Daddy grilled out, even when it was just hamburgers or hot dogs, the food was exceptional. Mama loved it, too, having a night off and thus eliminating the hellacious chore of thinking up a multicolored meal fit to eat.

You see, besides the notion of getting some action, a lot of men will cook if they can get away with boozing it up more than usual. The wife can't exactly count beer bottles when her husband is outdoors in the elements preparing the family's food. She's usually inside doing the salad. Or so it went in our household most weekends when Daddy took to the patio, his grill and his spirits.

Sometimes, he'd invite his men friends over and they'd reach inside a burlap sack bulging with raw oysters, cracking the shells and slurping the disgusting contents.

I remember the sack was almost as tall as I was, and wet with the smell of ocean seeping from what I thought bore too close a resemblance to phlegm for it to qualify as edible.

My mother and her women friends had no part of it. They stayed in the kitchen, not wanting to watch their husbands eat the things. They were Southern ladies wrapped in each other's drawling chitchat, their children somewhere outside packing dirt beneath their fingernails, mosquitoes welting their shins.

These women always retreated to the kitchen at the first mention of the burlap sack; they drank sweet tea and scrubbed potatoes for baking, rinsed shrimp they planned to boil, and talked about how in the world their husbands could eat raw oysters. Who in her right mind would eat them?

I've known a lot of women who will. Some say it's a great way to meet guys. Kind of like buying a truck or a bass boat. Do as they do and the men come clamoring, though personally, I'd rather be dateless and eating firm foods indigenous to land or air.

My sister and I dreaded the sight of that sweating bag of sea life, some of which we figured was still half-alive. We and the other kids would stare in transfixed horror as the men reached deeper. And then came the cracking and the shucking sounds followed by the disgusting slurps of our daddies entering mollusk heaven.

Every summer in southwest Georgia meant a chance to make as much money as we could stomach by eating raw oysters. Daddy and his buddies flipped quarters to the children who'd swallow the oysters and not run behind the house and upchuck.

No one would do it but me, because back in the sixties, a quarter went a long way. It bought a Coke and a Milky Way with a nickel to spare.

"I'll try one," I'd say, and the men smiled like adolescent boys pulling a prank.

My daddy would dig into that burlap bag and rustle around until he'd found a whopper, something that looked like a gnarled, webbed foot. He'd aim his little knife between the halves, and with a flick of his wrist, set the wiggling mass free.

"Here it is," he'd chime, sun and beer reddening his nose. "You sure about this? You 100 percent sure you want to try this?"

The other children would nudge me. "Go on, they're yummy," one boy had said, a real wimp who'd never eaten anything but chicken and tater tots in his entire life.

I'd held out my hand, and my father, as if a surgeon removing some tumor, gently lifted the gray matter and held it to my mouth. I opened enough to feel the cold wetness on my tongue and thought I'd pass out from the chill and texture. Surely this didn't qualify as a member of any food group.

I forced a smile and pretended to swallow. The men would clap, and as promised, hand over the quarter. I thought I'd die before enough time had passed that I could run behind the house and rid myself of what these fools called a delicacy.

Even so, it happened every summer. The oysters arrived. The men arrived. And I earned a single quarter.

My only comfort is that oysters take me back to Georgia, to the steaming summer nights and mosquito bites, the dirty nails and the smell of the beach right on our back porch.

* * *

Oysters and steaks aside, one of my dad's most beloved recipes is called Dusty's Chicken, named after our sweet neighbor in LaGrange, Georgia, a former football coach named Dusty Mills. People will look at the chicken strangely at first, because it's black and speckled, appearing more like cremated remains than dinner. The thing is, once you've convinced someone to try a delicious peg leg, you'll have to fight the rest of your life to get a fair share. They are swooningly divine.

Dusty's Chicken

Best to marinate this overnight.

Several pounds of chicken drummettes
1 cup Worcestershire sauce
1 cup ReaLemon Lemon Juice
1 Tbsp. salt
¼ cup vegetable oil

Mix this all together thoroughly and pour over the chicken.

Marinate overnight, turning several times. *(Do this even if you have to set the alarm and get out of bed. It will be worth it. I promise.)*

Grill 'til blackened.

Chicken isn't the only thing worthy of the grill masters. Men who eat meat like to believe they are kings of gas and charcoal when it comes to cooking steaks.

Grilling out is one of the staples of up to three seasons: spring, summer and fall, with steaks most likely to top the list of sizzling meats.

Cooking the perfect steak may sound easy, but it's more a combination of art and science than people realize. For beef eaters and steak lovers, here are some tips from pro grillers.

* * *

Gene Ellison—attorney, restaurant owner, basketball coach: Ellison is a man of many talents. He can cook, practice law and chat it up with just about anyone in town. Last week he treated his western North Carolina All-Stars, a team that won the state championship, to a cookout featuring his famous grilled rib eye recipe, one that will work for other cuts of beef as well.

The best steak for grilling, he says, is the rib eye, though even a New York Strip, when cooked properly is a tasty alternative. The key, he says, is not only in the preparation, but also in the cooking. Most people undermarinate and overcook. A delicious marinade and a few hours of soak time can turn even cheap beef cuts into gourmet morsels.

Here are tips from Ellison:

1. To get the best flavor from the meat, don't cook the steaks until they're done or they'll taste like rubber. Medium, or pink inside, makes for the best flavor, he said.

2. Prepare the grill. Not every grill was created equal.

   If using charcoal, let the carcinogenic properties burn off by lighting the grill and waiting a couple of hours prior to cooking.

   Gas may be simpler, but charcoal tastes better, he said.

3. The marinade can make or break the taste of a steak. Ellison reluctantly parts with his supersecret recipe.

Ellison's Secret Marinade

Best to marinate overnight.

Take 6 steaks, about 8 ounces each and not quite an inch thick

Create a marinade:
2 cups Worcestershire sauce
1½ cups soy sauce
½ cup red wine such as Merlot or Cabernet Sauvignon
1 Tbsp. onion, chopped
½ tsp. garlic, minced
1 bay leaf

"Now, here's the big secret," Ellison said. *"Emeril (the chef) does a steak rub."*

Take the meat before putting it in the marinade, and give it a firm rub all over, as if a massage.

"You can't go wrong," he said.

Marinate the steaks overnight in a sealed container.

Leftover Sauce

When it comes time for grilling, save the extra sauce.

Put the sauce on the stove and add a tablespoon of brown sugar, half a teaspoon of cracked black pepper and two pinches of ginger.

Boil this mixture on the stove.

In a separate bowl mix two teaspoons of cornstarch and six teaspoons of water. Turn down heat to simmer and gradually add the cornstarch mixture to thicken.

Ellison said this makes a great steak sauce.

Interesting facts from Ellison and Weber-Stephen Products Co.:

1. More women like their steaks well done and men prefer them rare.

2. Ellison knew a man back when the Peddler Steak House was open who'd eat a 32-ounce raw steak every time he visited.

3. More than half of all grill owners grill year-round.

4. About 70 percent use it once a week.

5. One in four men are more satisfied with their grilling style, saying they "are better than most."

6. Only 12 percent of women grillers claim the same.

7. About one-third of all grillers say they always or frequently over- or undercook their grilled food.

Can cheap meat taste great?

Yes. One doesn't have to buy filet mignon to enjoy a decent steak, Ellison said.

While he admits the best cuts are the filets, tenderloins, and rib eyes, New York Strips and T-bones, even flank and chuck roast steaks are good eating if properly cooked and seasoned.

CHAPTER THIRTEEN

Serve Ya a Meat, Ma'am?

If it weren't for cafeterias and covered-dish suppers, my kids would rarely have known certain vegetables existed. In particular, the kind that are all mushed up and blended with unrelated food items, namely in casseroles, which, in a kid's eyes, are nothing more than something resembling upchuck.

Children have yet to appreciate the beauty of cream of THIS and THAT soup and all the tricks the stuff can pull. All they see are bits of meat poking through yellow squash, crumbled RITZ Crackers, green beans and corn niblets covered in a beige paste, the most delicious known as cream of mushroom soup, a staple in my and every other Southern kitchen.

Then again, maybe they are actually smarter than us when they scream for mac and cheese and eschew the casserole concoctions.

What's even harder is trying to convince them to eat a congealed salad. I'm 46 years old and have a hard time swallowing a gelatinous mound that captures within its green membranes such fruits as ancient cherries and fuzzy grapes, plus nuts and other trapped and hairy items.

CAFETERIA TO THE RESCUE

Back when the kids were young and I fretted over their diets, my husband and I would load them up and hit the cafeterias. As many times as we've dined in such places, I've never quite pushed past the fear of the long line, the servers in their hairnets brandishing ultrahuge utensils and encouraging us to employ warp speed in making our selections. If I don't shout, "Fried chicken, white meat only" fast enough, I feel like I could be executed. SCHZZZZZ!

Each time we go, the fear is paralyzing and I freeze and babble while my husband huffs and ultimately makes the choices, goading me as one would an elderly deaf woman in a nursing home.

"Just pick a friggin' meat, would ya?" he says oh-so-romantically. "What's the problem? Get the damned Country-Fried Steak and move along. It's not rocket science."

"It's worse. What if I make the wrong choice? I hate having plate envy and wanting to pick off other's foods."

It's almost as if I'm a chameleon in a Crayola box and don't know which of the dozens of colors to choose. It would be nice and advisable to medicate oneself before entering one of these oft-slow-moving lines where many codgers, nursing home escapees and families of six to eight take forever to decide on a combination of foods, the din of "Vegetable, sir? Meat, ma'am?" blaring like human trumpets from the serving line.

How hard can it be to decide whether you want the Fried White Fish or the Cube Steak and Gravy? Why, it takes many people as long as it would at a sit-down restaurant, and meanwhile, you got people in line exhaling with exasperation and wetting their Depends. Not to mention those poor servers with their spatulas high in the air, ready to scoop a selection and plop it on a tray.

I know from personal experience that no matter what side

of the cafeteria line you're on—whether serving or being served—the experience raises blood pressures and can bring on palpitations. Every cafeteria should have some defibrillator paddles nearby or an IV drip of Valium.

One evening around seven, my family once again got up the nerve to hit a popular cafeteria near our house. Those in my region are mostly named with initials such as the J&S and the K&W, and then there's the one that tries to be more up-scale, the Piccadilly. I'd like to name such a place for what it really is: the S&M. Only sadists can eat there without having seizures.

While the four of us were there, the serving line had shrunk—enough so that people weren't sticking out the front doors, spilling their hunger into the parking lot and eager for the homemade cooking that pulls them from their own homes and E-Z Boys.

OK, I said to myself. I'm willing to go in and make a hard decision. They will not have to scream at me. I will know once I enter the line what I'm having, no wishy-washing. No imaginary stun guns pointed at my head by the hairnet crew.

It was a Friday night and my then-four-year-old was starved, and I didn't feel like cooking. Nothing new here. I could not in good conscience pour him yet another bowl of Lucky Charms. He needed vegetables, and no place but a cafeteria can get broccoli the texture my children will eat.

While cafeterias have long been known as the hangout for the older set, convening for a meal after their Bingo or Canasta games, I've begun noticing a younger crowd joining the regulars. Working parents and their tired brood find a cafeteria stop worth the price of not having to cook and wash dishes.

I became acquainted with cafeterias while living in Myrtle Beach, South Carolina, where a K&W stood a block from my house. I was dating my rich geriatric boyfriend who insisted he HAD to eat cafeteria food every day or he would up and die. At first, I thought I'd up and die going through the line and being squawked at by the loud hawk- and falconlike employees foisting meats and vegetables on us faster than our eyes could blink.

In a split second, my eyeballs burning red, the employees forced me to choose between roast beef and fried chicken, between a vegetable medley and a sweet potato.

I learned to view the cafeterias as the great marathons of eating. You queue up to the starting line, and prepare for hell. People love these places. Once I'm in line, I do some stretching and deep breathing, so as not to pass out upon entering the metal gates of quick decisions.

I've begun a new trick of staring at others' plates while twenty feet away, thus trying to decide what to eat a good half hour before my time to spit out selections.

Strategy One: Plate Watching

Plate watching is a sport that can make or break a dining selection. You can also analyze people, such as potential suitors, by becoming a well-trained plate watcher, and there's no better place to plate watch than a cafeteria.

I believe you can tell more about people by observing how and what they eat than if they'd filled out an endless psychological profile.

My sister gave me the nickname of Plate Watcher years ago. She says during dinner I roll my eyes like a hoot owl's and cast glances from side to side, lighting upon the various platters and their owners.

"You just need to worry about your own food," she'd snarl, peering at her dinnerware as if it were some kind of inner mirror. "It makes people nervous when you stare at their food. It's doglike."

She had a full-size dish, and on it her selections seemed lost: a tablespoon of peas, half a dollop of mashed potatoes, a serving of pot roast the size of two quarters, and a pear salad minus the cheese and mayonnaise.

She once was a small woman, not much bigger than part of an Olsen twin. I have learned by watching her eat that, like most of us, she fears fat. She slowly nips at her toddler-size servings and pushes away from the table with a satiated groan.

"I think I'll go train for my marathon," she'd announce as I rose for seconds.

As for my mother, Lord! She'll load her plate until not a speck of china shows. Or, if it's not a special occasion, we'll eat from the Gulf dishes. (Note: We call them the Gulf dishes because years ago, back in LaGrange, Georgia, she'd whip her Cutlass Supreme into the Gulf gas station and receive a free plate with every fill-up.)

She also owns remnants of a beautiful stemware collection, compliments of DUZ detergent, an ancient brand few probably recall. I remember Mama bringing a new box home every week and rushing to dig through the granules until she discovered the buried glass.

Mama's plate is always a bounty. After the blessing, she forgets there's a mountain of food in front of her and chatters until it grows cold and stiff. By the meal's end, she may have managed four or five bites.

She's as skinny as an old man's belt and not afraid to top off her supper with a REESE'S Cup. She's just one of those lucky people for whom food isn't the magic elixir, a solvent for stress.

Next comes my dad. He begins his meal with a huge salad, a crunching, deafening display of a man chasing health. Afterward, he moves to the meat and potatoes, methodically clicking and scraping his fork. He'll spend glorious minutes piling and aligning food items, inching them loudly toward the outer edges of his plate. It is at this point my mother gives me a look that says, "Keep your cool. He's the only daddy you have."

Once finished, he'll grab a yeast-swollen biscuit or box of Cheez-Its and slink away toward the TV room so he doesn't have to face me, the Plate Watcher. Later, feeling guilty just because he was raised to, he'll walk up hills in the neighborhood, burning calories until his hip hurts, then come home and fall asleep in front of the TV.

Being a Plate Watcher is a joyful hobby, one that has served me well. Here is what I've learned:

A. My sister is a knockout for whom food is a necessary evil, an enemy always out to get her. She needs to heed my motto: Nobody wants a bone but a dog. (Note: Since getting rid of her first husband, who liked his women thin as stick bugs and bulging with fake teats, Sister Sandy is eating fine and her weight is normal.)

B. My mother could care less about food, but loves her plates and glasses, a woman more into free tableware than she is a Sunday dinner.

C. My father is aware of every bite, a disciplined man who lines up his life just as he lines up his food.

Everything with a proper place. Everything in order.

This is exactly why I stare at everyone's plates in restaurants and cafeterias. It's a curiosity, but more than that a hobby, a study into a person's soul and desires.

The mother lode of plate watching can be accomplished at cafeterias. And even though they cause me heaps of stress with the barking of questions and pressure to pick a meat quicker than one can say "burger," I've never met a cafeteria I didn't like. Not even the loud, noisy ones where servers blast questions as far down the line as the human voice carries.

As I stood in line with my son who was climbing the railings and causing a few patrons to give me the eye, I analyzed plates, most of which were piled with artery-clogging lumps, gravies, breads and rich pies.

By the time someone hollered, "Meat, ma'am?" I'd panicked. All those juicy combinations I'd seen rolling down the serving line were wiped from my memory. I was drawing a blank.

"Meat, WOMAN!" the server screamed again.

"Umm. Well . . . I, uh . . ."

"MEAT?" She purely trembled like an angry hedgehog.

"I . . . Just . . . just give me the chicken."

"We have three kinds. Didn't you study the lineup prior to getting to this point?"

I felt my legs grow weak and floated into a stress-induced flashback.

It was October 9, 1992, at six AM, and I was lying in the operating room of a local hospital awaiting a C-section. For some reason I turned toward my husband, terrified, but with an odd thought. He was wearing a mask, hairnet and scrubs and looked as if he needed a carving knife.

"Serve you a meat?" I asked, through the haze of an epidural.

The doctor and attendants began laughing.

The flashback ended when a woman pitching entrées gave up on me and yelled, "Meat!" to the next in line.

Then another server's eyes bored into me, giant utensil in her hand as she squawked, "VEGETABLE, MA'AM?"

"Is Valium a vegetable?"

She clicked her spoon hard against the metal tray and ignored me.

A few days later, like a heat-seeking missile, I was back. Different cafeteria, same procession of questions:

"Meat? Vegetable? Bread?"

I took time to chat with an employee, a veteran of the line at this J&S.

"I have a lot of fun with the customers," said Nancy, a line supervisor.

The manager said he's seen it all during his years as a cafeteria man. He remembers a busy Sunday afternoon when the endless line finally thinned. A man with a strange expression on his face approached him.

"May I speak to you a second?" the guy asked.

"Sure. Why not."

"There's a pair of ladies' underwear on the floor over there," he said.

"What?" The cafeteria manager thought he'd heard incorrectly.

The man led him to a spot in line where panties the size of a parachute lay crumpled.

"Apparently the elastic broke," the manager said, face red as watermelon. "We see everything here. We just try to have good, clean fun while out there working."

I remembered this conversation when it came time for me to perhaps consider a career other than writing for newspapers. I'd been in the news business for twenty-five years, and while loving it, hit a snag and suffered burnout. All kinds of careers went through my head: Gap saleslady, Planet Smoothie shake maker, nurse's aide and cafeteria worker (due to the free food I would get).

I called the manager of our local cafeteria, a huge operation with restaurants in other cities, and asked if I could come and serve.

"Don't worry," I said. "I don't want to get paid. I just want to see what it's like on the OTHER SIDE. I promise not to sue for injury or hold you accountable for anything that may transpire including my expiring over one of the hot trays of mashed potatoes."

"Type up a waiver and come on over," he said. "We'll put you on the line."

The next day I stood amid steaming vapors and smells of homemade cooking, put on the hairnet and looked in the mirror, aghast. I had been whupped with a giant Ugly Stick. Wearing gloves, the net and an apron, I worked alongside two employees who'd each been there twenty years or more.

The manager had told me the goal was to move at least 150 people an hour through the line as fast as possible without actually lassoing them. Each person represents an average of $7 spent.

Speed, he said, is the foundation on which cafeterias make their money. Slow down the line and the system collapses.

With no training whatsoever, I stood behind the silver trays of meats, vegetables, casseroles, freshly baked pies and rolls. My stomach growled as the guests piled their plates with all sorts of food choices I deemed my business to critique.

My plate-watching disorder kicked in at full throttle.

"Ma'am, you may want to put something green on that tray. It looks awfully brown with all that gravy. You know my mama used to make brown meals and—"

Beverly, my "coworker," elbowed me and shook her head. The woman in line stared as if a rock had hit her. The Golden Rule in the cafeteria business is stick to the code language, which includes, "Serve you a meat? Vegetable, sir? What are you having, miss? Tarter or coleslaw with that fish, hon?"

Beverly replaced a tray of empty green beans and said, "We aren't even supposed to say 'hon' or 'sugar,' but I've been saying it for years."

I'd work at a cafeteria forever if I could stand by Beverly the entire shift. She never corrected me when I'd venture from the short script. I felt as if everyone else behind the line had a job. Some were salad chefs, some meat tenders, while the others served beverages, vegetables, desserts or breads. No one was dispensing nutritional counseling, which I felt certain was desperately needed and so I gave myself that position.

These lost souls with brown meals needed a food coach, and I decided that since the other workers had the meats and vegetable orders served long before the folks reached the breads area, that's where I'd give my unsolicited counseling.

"You got two starches on your plate, sir, and even though

we don't use animal fats in our dishes, you might want to re-think asking for a roll made of white flour."

His face twisted into a grimacing expression as if an attack of angina had hit. "Just a friendly suggestion," I said and smiled, but it didn't work because I wasn't cute enough in a hairnet to get away with this nonsense. Had the hairnet not been part of the uniform, I'd have stood a much better chance of charming them all into well-balanced meals.

The manager walked up behind me just as I was saying, "You're what? Not having a vegetable! Ma'am, the government's panel of foodies highly suggests three to five servings of fruits and vegetables a day and I don't see a single piece of fruit on your—"

"Shhhh. Don't make conversation with the customers," the manager said as politely as possible. "Stick to 'What are you having?' or 'Serve you a meat?'"

The script is in place for a reason. Move 'em in, get 'em out. Cafeterias are no place for fraternizing with the behind-the-scenes help. Nor should servers try to be anything but human spatulas and forks, albeit pleasant.

I couldn't help myself. "Beverly, how in the world can people eat this way? Don't they know it'll kill them?"

She laughed and said a man comes in regularly who asks her to carve only the gooey layer of fat from the top of the roast. That hunk of clear fat is all he eats.

I'm sure the man is a widower because they are the types who've been harped at for years concerning their diets, and when the wife finally dies, they go wild and eat anything they want.

When the manager left, I spotted a poor woman with nothing on her plate but a piece of fried fish.

"Turnips are filled with vitamins A and E and would complement your pan-fried trout beautifully," I said.

She flared her nostrils. "Turnips are for hillbillies."

"Well, how about this nice broccoli? You could get it without the cheese sauce? Perhaps top it all off with a whole wheat roll, skip dessert and call it a successful meal."

Beverly's eyes popped as I counseled the woman. "You're going to get us all fired," she said, laughing.

"OK. I'll stop. Listen, I'm curious. Has anything strange ever happened to the people in line?"

She carefully carved the roast in ultrathin slices as she considered the question. "I've seen them drop dead before they could make it to the salads," she said matter-of-factly. "Not just one, but several in my twenty years here working the line."

I wondered had any of the guests been mean to Beverly, who was purely filled with joy and sweetness. When she said, "Vegetable?" it was as if she was saying, "I love and care about you." That's just how she is.

"I was calling vegetables one day," she said, "and some woman cussed me out and said I sounded like an army recruiter. And lots of times you get cussed out if you don't give them enough food."

"I guess I could see that happening." Just five minutes earlier I'd told an elderly man that he'd be seeing "Jesus, or the other dude, real soon" if he dared to pair that double-chocolate pie with his fried chicken.

"You're asking for a coronary or a big old aneurysm," I said and winked, hoping the wink would signify my deep care and concern. When a woman in a hairnet winks, it's not sexy.

"I think that's something I'll decide for myself," he snapped. "Why don't you take your business out of my one pleasurable meal of the day?"

"Yes, sir. I just wanted you to live to see plenty of holidays. The government's guidelines suggest—"

"Screw the hell out of the government," he said and disappeared into the dining room, fluffy pie on his tray.

After "working" the line for about an hour, my back began to ache and I felt bad for those who had to stand there for eight hours. I removed my apron, hairnet and gloves and called it a day, leaving with a lot of respect for these dedicated souls who serve the people and then bite their tongues about giving nutritional advice or engaging in any kind of chitchat whatsoever.

"You've lasted longer than some of our new hires," Beverly said, laughing, a giant spoon in one hand poised to attack the new batch of mashed potatoes.

We hugged good-bye. That's how wonderful these people are. They are huggers, and anyone who hugs is an all-round good person. Of course, I'm not talking about choir directors who molest young boys or other pedophiles and sex offenders. I mean regular people.

A hug is like a gift. And so is nutritional counseling in a cafeteria, though no one else sees it that way.

CHAPTER FOURTEEN

Cutthroat Covered-Dish Suppers

There's an old saying about sin and salvation. If the lost and troubled really want to get to Heaven, it helps to know the secret password.

COVERED DISH.

Just show up with your Pyrexes packed with macaroni pie and the pearly gates will open wide. The Lord and every church this side of Asia lives and thrives on covered-dish suppers. Even Yankees partake, calling them "potlucks."

They are a Southern staple—but they are much more than about the food. There's an underlying psychology behind each dish and its maker.

Take one Sunday a few years ago.

Mama and her older sister, my wild Aunt Betty, had discovered a small Baptist church on the outskirts of Spartanburg, South Carolina. Aunt Betty, who works in a furniture store, met the new preacher while he, too, was selling Posturepedics. It was as good a time as any for these two sisters to dust off their Bibles and reacquaint themselves with the Lord.

They'd raised children and lived through their offsprings' births and divorces. The gray hairs were coming on fast, the wrinkles even faster and time passed like a deck of flushed cards. Get to know Jesus now, or miss the train to Heaven.

That's why so many blue-heads (and I plan to be one) darken the doors every Sunday and Wednesday (if you're Baptist).

For the church homecoming each year Mama and Aunt Betty would spend all of Saturday making green bean and squash casseroles, deviled eggs and potato salads. Even my daddy got involved, rising early Sunday morning and firing up the grill so the good Baptists would have hot, charbroiled chicken drummettes, called "Dusty's Chicken" (see Chapter Twelve for the recipe).

When we arrived at the church, at least a dozen tables strained under the weight of everyone's labors.

"Goodness," I said. "I've never seen this much food in all my life." My eyes settled on a beautiful Red Velvet Cake in the lineup of sinful chocolate cakes and pies.

"Well, I just hope they eat these peg legs your daddy spent all morning cooking," Mama said, arranging her food toward the end of the table she assumed would be the start of the serving line. "That's his contribution to the Lord. I can't get him to join on the dotted line, but he'll feed the flock and the children and cart them all hither and yon. He gives everything but his signature because he knows Jesus keeps the real scorecard and not the church secretary."

During the sermon, as the preacher spoke of everlasting life, I couldn't stop thinking about Red Velvet Cake. Finally, the last hymn sung, we convened for the feast.

"Time to enjoy the fruits of God's and the good people of this church's efforts. Let the covered dish commence," the reverend said after properly (and lengthily) blessing the food.

Mama's face fell when she saw the line forming on the opposite end of the table, the end not laden with her and Daddy's efforts. And let me tell you, a woman who spends a Saturday morning with her hair splattered in cream of mushroom soup wants to make sure she takes home an empty dish.

My great-grandmother, who presided over many a covered-dish supper, used to oooh and ahhh over her own creations, pretending they were someone else's, telling people, "You really need to try that congealed salad," and, "Jesus strike me dead on the spot if those aren't the best limas you ever put in your mouth."

Mama frowned at the untouched peg legs, pouted that the little drummettes, looking for all the world as if rescued from a blazing fire, were going untouched. Why, people stared at them and audibly said, "Ewwwh!" If you ask me, that's not churchyfied behavior.

"Nobody's eating that chicken," she bemoaned, her mind working, coming up with a "Covered Dish Plan of Action."

The lovely lady seated across from us got up, leaving her plate unattended. Mama eyed that half-empty plate and slipped out of her seat. She lined her purse with a napkin, snuck down to the end of the table and grabbed some of Daddy's cremated chicken drummettes. She dumped all she could into her Liz Claiborne bag, as if she were a little old lady sprung from a nursing home, wondering where the next decent meal might be found. She returned to the table grinning and all but laughing in the house of the Lord.

"Susan," she whispered. "Listen up and don't say a word. You hear me? Do Not Laugh. I need you to put these peg legs on Eunice's plate, then go around and when people aren't looking, give them at least three of these. They're scared to eat them because they're black. They don't realize that's the sauce. They think they're burned up, and I don't want them to go to waste."

"Mama!"

"Oh, just do it."

When Eunice returned, she scanned her plate and reached for a charred leg, then withdrew her hand as if touching a snake.

I couldn't resist. "Ummm. Those chicken legs sure are good. I wonder who in the world made this blackened fowl."

Eunice seemed puzzled. "Why, I don't know. Somebody dumped them on my plate," she said. "I know I only got two meats. Not three."

I laughed and didn't stop until my teeth ached and tears spilled from my eyes. Mama tried to shrink in her chair, and Aunt Betty roared, pound cake sputtering from her lips. "P-Pe-Peg!" she coughed and blew crumbs. "You're a-aw-awful."

The poor Eunice woman kept her eye on the black meat, as if trying to will it away with enough pupil power.

"It was Mama's idea," I told Ms. Eunice and felt my mother's famous twisteroo pinch tug mightily at my side meat. I jerked away and scooted my chair closer to Eunice's. "Ya see? Mama means well and only wanted everybody to eat Daddy's peg legs. I gotta get up now and sneak a few on the other people's plates when they aren't looking."

Mama turned red and made an evil and unchristian face at me. "I know they look bad," she explained to those nearby with the charred flesh on their Chinets, "but they really are delicious. It's the secret sauce that makes them look burned up."

Just then another church lady stopped by our table.

"I bet you got some of that good coconut cake, didn't you?" she asked Eunice, the woman with the newly acquired drummettes. I had seen that very lady carefully removing the coconut cake from her silver Buick, and knew she was the cook behind the frosting. Dang, all the women were in on this old scheme of trying to be the Darling of the Covered Dish.

"No, Sugar Tit," Eunice said to the woman, using a common Southern expression. (Everyone special is called Sugar Tit by old ladies.) "I didn't try the cake, but somehow I ended up with these chicken legs I'm going to need a set of vaccinations to swallow."

She turned toward my mother, winked and hee-hawed, wrapping a leg in a napkin, promising to eat it later.

"The Lord must have let you dump these old things in the right place."

Mama doubted she would really eat it later. I saw her eyeing the podium at the end of the room, noticing there was a microphone and small public address system nearby.

"Oh, no," I said. "You're not getting up and making an announcement about these chicken legs. I will leave and not come back to get you."

She turned to me. "Well then, Miss Priss who cooked nothing for Jesus! Get up now and start distributing those legs." It wasn't easy, let me tell you, to slip from chair to chair and spill a trio of charcoal-colored drummettes onto people's plates. I managed to get rid of about two dozen until the preacher caught me.

"What are you doing?"

"Serving the Lord," I said. "Giving people a little extra because I know deep down they are hungry and don't want to appear greedy. Gluttony is a sin. So is sloth. Or rather being a sloth or . . . adultery . . . murder . . . coveting thy neighbor's covered dishes."

This new preacher walked away baffled. When he returned to his Chinet, Mama had three peg legs waiting.

At these events, some cooks will spend hours on their offerings and concoct foods guaranteed to bring people clamoring for recipes. Others, like me, will say, "I'll be happy to bring the napkins and a couple of liters of Coke and Sprite. Or if some emphysemic wants a pack of Camels, I wouldn't mind springing for those."

The thing is, since joining the Read It Or Not, Here We Come Book Club, each month guests are expected to either whip up an appetizer or entrée. I am blown away by some of their exquisite, 5-star-quality recipes. For me, a working mom, I typically stop by the Fresh Market—a gourmet and quite uppity grocery store—and buy a tub of their delicious pimiento cheese and maybe a box of high-end crackers from lands overseas.

During the few times I've been inspired to actually turn on a burner and pull out ingredients for a meal, it hasn't gone well. This is why I've invented a way to "slip" a dish into the lineup while no one else notices.

What you do is keep your dish or item under wraps and wait until all the ladies have gone into another room for seating and drinking, then push your goods in the center of the pile so they get lost among the better choices.

If you're lucky, not a soul will say, "Who brought the 80-bean salad?" (This is my most embarrassing yet colorful dish that consists of every bean known to womankind, a dish I nicknamed "Clean Bean Salad," since it involves ransacking the shelves of the pantry and opening every can one can find, dousing the entire mixture with a bottle of Seven Seas Italian Dressing.)

While the book club members are raving about one another's dishes, I claim nothing unless asked and then, if pressed, I mumble and point blindly at the table.

"What did you bring, Susan?" one of the more outspoken members, my dear friend Sandy, who is in dire need of some hormone therapy, might ask.

I stare at the delicacies and nod toward the one that looks most appealing. "That," I'll say.

"Try again. I made that last night."

"OK. The chips. There, you happy?"

At every covered dish or potluck I attend, I'm typically in such a hurry, the opportunity to shine as a chef is short-circuited in the name of time, and the grocery deli is my best friend. The thing is, most people can detect deli food a mile away, especially if it's from your average grocery store where everything is eerily similar in taste to junior high lunches.

If push comes to major shove and I have to SHINE at one of these things—say, it's the company's summer picnic and the evil boss will reign over the buffet line until the last dish is tagged and turned in, I have to go all out and make the one thing I know will be a major hit. I usually don't fix it because it involves a lot of chopping and ingredients, and of course precious hours out of one's day.

Here is my one and only recipe of delectability, guaranteed to please most. I stole this from another woman who'd brought it to a 12-Step meeting's New Year's potluck.

Oriental Noodle Salad

2 or 3 packages of Ramen noodles, any flavor
¾ cup slivered or sliced almonds
½ cup margarine or butter
1 or 2 bags of broccoli slaw. *(The original recipe calls for a head of Foxy Napa Cabbage, but I usually can't find it, and when I do, it scares me half to death, the way it looks like collards.)*
Sesame seeds *(unless they give you gas).*

Melt the margarine/butter and add the crushed noodles. *(Yes, I forgot. You have to crush them up.)*
Toss in the almonds and brown the mixture. Set aside.
Add one bunch of green onions, diced, and one red pepper, chopped. *(Don't be cheap and get a green pepper. The red ones MAKE the dish.*

Dressing
¾ cup olive oil
½ cup sugar
¼ cup white vinegar

Bring above ingredients to a boil and stir in two tablespoons soy sauce and one of Worcestershire sauce. Cool. Then pour over noodle mixture.

This stuff is sooooo good, my in-laws and I started eating it for breakfast, lunch and dinner. It's really addictive and, unfortunately, a toot producer. (Tooting is the polite way of saying "fart.") While it's a bit difficult for the kitchen virgin's repertoire, this dish is doable and one that seasoned cooks would call a simple recipe.

If you've prepared this salad, you can go to any covered dish or potluck supper and proudly and loudly announce your item has arrived and place it center stage on the table. I've even been known to stand next to my huge bowl of Oriental Noodle Salad and personally serve my friends and guests, to ensure they try it, but more than that, to make certain they know I made it.

CHAPTER FIFTEEN

If Your Kids Like School Lunches, You Suck as a Cook

At night, long after everyone is in bed, I creep to the kitchen to do something I genuinely dread, something I swore I would never do.

I prepare school lunches.

I take out bags of bread and free the slices with a flick of the twist ties. Carefully, I pull out four pieces, hoping the mold and hardness of time haven't struck. I open jars of Peter Pan, packs of honey-smoked turkey, cabinets and pantries and the refrigerator until the entire kitchen counter bustles like a midnight diner.

Just before doing this, I read the school lunch menu printed biweekly on colorful paper, praying for a few pizza days or, at the very least, crossing my fingers for something my fourth-grader will eat, thus preventing this task that steals the evening's final hour. Ha! And husbands wonder why they aren't "getting any."

Mothers everywhere pack lunches when half-dead with sleep, but some of them seem to take great pleasure in seeing how Martha Stewarty they can get. I mentioned in an earlier chapter the mom who always made her twins' French toast and bacon, tucked into their Louis Vuitton lunch box (or some such designer contraption) a linen napkin, with a ring, and mini bottles of real Vermont maple syrup. Forget Aunt Jemima.

Other mothers, faced with the daunting task of assembling decent lunches, pray the strawberries aren't moldy, knowing our kids won't eat them but the teachers will notice our attention to detail and the government's recommendations for three to five servings of fruits and vegetation daily. We toss in yogurt and apple slices, which will turn brown by lunchtime unless we squirt lemon juice on them, rendering them sour and inedible. It's like you can't win.

There are pita pockets to stuff, angels and stars to cut from plain sandwich bread if a diva dwells in the house for whom squares aren't worthy. There are GLAD bags and tiny Rubbermaid containers, and I fill each one with things my kids may or may not eat, but appear presentable enough to keep teachers from calling the food-pyramid police.

Plenty of us worry what the teachers will think of our lunches.

Back when I obsessed and cared too much, before drifting off to sleep, while in that gauzy state of existence, I'd imagine their conversations. "That Reinhardt woman sent her child ashy carrots yesterday. You know them ashy kind? Been in the fridge two years? Last week her poor child had mold on her blueberries. Hell, just pack their little asses a Pop-Tart if you can't keep your vegetation up-to-date."

This movement to pack a lunch is a growing trend and wasn't part of my life as a child. Ninety percent of us ate what the hardworking lunch ladies had prepared, no matter that much of it was unidentifiable during the era thirty and forty years ago when government's eyes weren't so watchful over what the schools served their charges.

Some meals were good, well, at least the rolls were. And some were a force to be digested with. If the food wasn't scrumptious, the smells from the cafeteria always were. Scents of baking bread spread a feeling of love and home all the way to gym class where we jumped rope and threw softballs as far as they would go.

The cafeteria at my all-girls junior high meant ladies in hairnets and industrial white body aprons, spooning potpies and spaghetti balls, corn and green beans, and various casseroles from gleaming silver pans. Many of these ladies would smile like beloved grandmothers. Others seemed as mysterious as the gravy-smothered meats they served.

I remember being afraid at times to look at the lunch ladies directly, as if they held an intangible power in their trays and big spoons, their gloved hands glistening with the steam from hot dishes coming and going from the cavernous, clanking kitchens.

My own mother, no matter how much my sister and I might complain, was never one to pack lunches. Oh, when we were in first grade, she bought us a lunch box, but only once or twice did she ever fill it with things from her own kitchen.

She wanted us to have what she referred to as a "hot meal."

Truthfully, after eating the bologna sandwiches she packed a few times, the scent of the meat overpowering by lunchtime during those days pre-coolers, I never wanted a lunch from home.

Though I didn't want to hurt her feelings, I actually thought the food at school was pretty good. Sure, there was the occasional plop of hominy grits, a knee-buckling bad starch of some sort and a few other inedible oddities that ended up on those delightful compartmentalized trays.

I vowed when I had kids of my own, they, too, would eat the school lunches. I'd tell them how wonderful they were, and how a peanut butter and jelly sandwich or nitrate-infiltrated lunchmeats would lead to cancerous tumors or atrophied muscles.

"What's atrophied?" they might ask.

"Means the muscles rot from bone."

My son, however, didn't fully buy this line of thinking, and I acquiesced and caved to his requests of lunch packing.

Every evening, before the dreaded ritual of brown bagging, I'd try to convince him about the wonders of Salisbury Steak, the joy of "Manager's Choice."

"LUNCHABLES, please," he'd say, wanting that overpriced premade concoction of preservative-infused coldcuts and cheese.

My children didn't know it at the time, but in my mind, once they reached middle school, which presented more dining options, the home kitchen was shutting down after supper.

Back when I was in elementary school, only the prissiest, sickliest and porkiest kids brought lunches from home, nestled and souring in metal boxes that said Barbie or Batman.

The rest of us, whether our mothers could cook or not, were expected to partake of the cafeteria selections, much of which was curious fare similar to what's served in the worst soup kitchens or prisons.

To be politically correct and in all honesty, schools have worked diligently with their boards and higher-ups to revamp menus and create palatable, if not downright semidelicious offerings.

This is but a fairly recent swing to decent things. We know all too well the gooey blobs gelling on plastic trays served back in the sixties and into the seventies.

As for my second born . . . When she started kindergarten I vowed to end my late-night lunch packing and prepare her with heavy fibbing as to the utter culinary pleasures of the school cafeteria.

"Children who don't eat school lunches grow up with a higher likelihood of breaking bones and getting acne," I'd say. "They're also more likely not to get invited to all the good birthday parties." Boy, I was mean.

Or maybe this: "I knew a girl whose mama packed her a lunch of sandwiches and sugar cookies every day and she ended up weighing 400 pounds and couldn't go to recess. Every tooth in her head fell out or turned black."

*   *   *

Sometimes in life, there's no choice, no cafeteria, no lunch ladies or giant kitchens. The only option is to let the kids starve or scramble for a half-decent bagged lunch.

Take summer camps and preschools. I have a friend who e-mailed all tizzyfied because she had to pack her cherub a lunch for summer camp every day. Since there wasn't even access to a microwave, she wrestled with trying to fix an appealing lunch that wouldn't involve teachers calling Social Services.

I imagined such a call. "Got one on the line, Martha," a voice says. "Little Tots Day Care says she ain't putting greens and yellows in her chirren's lunches. Send someone out pronto and give that woman a giant poster of the food pyramid."

My friend contacted me fretting and wondering what, besides Lunchables, she might possibly stuff in her daughter's box.

She would love a grocery list that included all the basics one might need for a week's worth of poke. She seemed to think I would know this offhand. Bless her heart.

Here's what I say to packing lunches: If you have to do it, say for camp, special events or preschools with no kitchens, then do it. Toss in a few carrots and berries for color and to keep the teachers from saying horrible things behind your back. Throw in a grilled cheese or peanut butter sandwich shaped from cookie cutters if the kid has the Great Fear of Bread Crusts.

Drop in an orange you know will never be peeled, and then smile. Send her off. If she gets hungry, she'll eat. If not, she'll trade.

Here's what I recently told my own baby love, the child I prepared early for the delights of the school cafeteria.

"Sug," I said, "just you wait. They have the best food in the world. Better than the Piccadilly." She didn't see my crossed fingers. I tried to envision the one or two memories of school lunches from the seventies that were actually pretty recognizable and tasty, wanting to fire her up for the thrill of the square tray and baby milk carton.

"They have the most wonderful Jell-O," I said. "Oh, honey, it has things inside of it that may look hairy but I assure you they are a real treat. And wait till you taste the Spaghetti Ball. They use some sort of ice-cream scooper and a perfect sphere of spaghetti lands right on your plate. No loose noodles. Everything packed into one scrumptious lump.

"Oh, and if you eat the fabulous Succotash—a carnival of color that includes all sorts of vegetables—they'll give you a giant sugar cookie. There's really nothing quite as adventurous as school lunches, honey. Remember, the kids who take their lunches are pure wimps, and I know you don't want to be like that. You buck up and eat the rice balls and mystery steaks. You may come home with bad breath, but it sure beats a tuna sandwich that has festered for four hours in a Barbie lunch box."

She stared at me with the same look she has been tossing for years: the "My mother is a bona-fide . . ." expression.

One of my friends who grew up in rural Tennessee recently reminisced about his own days of eating his hot meals at school.

"They still give 'em Cowboy Hats?" he asked, trying to talk like a hick to match the food he was discussing. "That there's your fried baloney with a big old scoop of cold, congealed instant mashed potatoes in the middle, and some Velveeta on top."

"We didn't have those in Georgia," I told him.

"I sure hope your daughter don't get no Cowboy Hats," he said. "It'll ruin her. She'll cry and beg every night that you pack her a sweet little lunch or she'll just starve to death."

I tried to picture these Cowboy Hats, and for some reason, I believed that would be the one food she'd enjoy.

In order to help other mothers who despise packing lunches, here are some sample menus for my fellow kitchen virgins, lunches that will both please the child and the teachers who'll no doubt peep into the lunch box and pass a slice of judgment.

Lunchables With Merit

OK, you're exhausted and the LUNCHABLES were on sale two-for-one. Go ahead and buy a few. The top choice for me would be the Cracker Stackers, which include a ham and turkey with a cracker and cheese combination. Something about a cold hot dog or pizza kit seems both disgusting and challenging for little digestive systems.

To its credit, the Kraft company is creating new and more nutritious products each year, so there may come a time when we'll never have to do the old bread 'n' spread routine again.

Place the LUNCHABLE in a very cute and CLEAN lunch container.

Add baby carrots. *(If you're really paranoid, get the organic kind and leave them in the bag so the teacher will see* ORGANIC *marked on the package.)*

Throw in a shiny Red Delicious or Granny Smith apple. *Of course, the kids will take one bite and discard it, but it's only for show, anyway.*

Add a granola or cereal bar *(so the kid doesn't starve).*

Pack a juice box, one with 100 percent real fruit juice. Or a Yoo-hoo. *Believe it or not, Yoo-hoos have calcium.*

CHAPTER SIXTEEN

Before SPAM Hit Computers,
It Was a Meat to Be
Reckoned With

I grew up in the sixties and seventies and we ate a lot of SPAM. Certain people have no idea what SPAM is, and probably think it's a constant cyber barrage of penis-enlargement ads.

Long before mass e-mails soliciting money (SPAM) for falsely imprisoned foreign dignitaries, a humble little meatlike product called SPAM hit the shelves and bellies of people everywhere.

Chances are, if you grew up in Georgia or any of the other Southern states, you're familiar with this cheap, stomach-filling product.

No one back then asked, "What's in this stuff?" or "How many fat grams does it contain?"

SPAM is a food product, a meat by-product made by the Hormel Company that comes in a tin and is some sort of multi-processed substance. SPAMsperts (experts in the tinned-meat world) have sworn if not for SPAM, plenty of soldiers in war days would have starved or come down with rickets from lack of protein. At the end of World War II, people even distributed SPAM to help feed the starving folks in Europe.

SPAM tends to divide people into three groups—those who love it, those who hate it and those who refuse to find out, according to a recent article by the Associated Press.

"Wherever you fall, it's almost hard not to respect—or at least be in awe of—a 'meat product' that's been around for 70 years," the AP said. "And to mark its platinum anniversary, SPAM is rolling out single-serve packets of its signature product. That's right, no more fussing with a can. SPAM aficionados now can get their fix in 3-ounce packets in either Classic or Lite (half the fat, a third fewer calories, a quarter less sodium).

"But perhaps more interesting than the food contained in the packets is the campy verbiage on the outside. 'This dotted line is like a freeway,' the package of SPAM Single-Serving reads along the tear-to-open-here line. 'The freeway to a delicious explosion in your mouth.'

"Or this on the SPAM Lite Single packet: 'It's time to enjoy. Take another bite and throw your head back and think wonderful thoughts of faraway places while you chew. Like a magical SPAM Lite castle in the sky . . .' "

GAWD FORBID!!!!

Now back to Reality:

Surprisingly, many of my own native people don't know what SPAM is, what's in it or anything about this processed product. I grew up falsely thinking it was a concoction of pork and pork guts and grossness like pig anuses, snouts and lips, and any other undesirable part of the porker.

Now you can get turkey SPAM, low-sodium SPAM and other more healthful varieties. The things that have remained constant are that it's cheap, like Ramen noodles, and offers protection against starvation and protein deficiencies.

"It's a delicacy in Hawaii," said Allen Boyd, the giant man who makes Al's Bad-Ass Wings and Big Al's Redneck Spaghetti (see recipes, Chapter 8).

My mother could take a can of SPAM, as did many moms of that era, and turn it into a nice piece of crisp "meat" to be eaten as a sandwich or a stand-alone with pintos and plenty of onions to kill the flavor or texture.

Mama would fry SPAM in butter until it burned. Burned meant nice and crunchy and rendered us amnesiacs to the parts of the pig we were eating. Not that we knew or cared, any more than we did about what's really in a hot dog. We were too dumb to know any better and thought it was a special and delectable treat.

I thought SPAM was a dying dish until Leah McGrath, a lovely and very healthy dietician for a major chain of grocery stores, invited me to join her in judging the Great American SPAM Championship at the North Carolina Mountain State Fair.

"Don't eat a bite of breakfast," Leah, also a food purist, health nut and buffet-a-phobe, advised. "This is something we must steel our stomachs to handle."

While it wasn't the breakfast of champions, SPAM dishes kept the judges entertained and gagging for water for hours.

The twenty-seven chefs, ranging in age from 6 to 60-something, had whipped up SPAM-packed recipes I'd have never thought possible. These were nothing shy of artistic feats, catapulting SPAM into new culinary heights.

My personal favorites, tastewise, didn't win. They included the Hot and Spicy Sizzlin' SPAM Fajitas and the SPAM Alfredo. We had to judge based not only our tastes buds but also on presentation and originality.

We ate SPAM every which way, including loose and floating in a SPAM minestrone.

A few other good recipes included Cowboy Caviar, a spread of cream cheese, green onions, Duke's mayo, shredded SPAM and fresh chives. This stuff swiped on Captain's Wafers could have passed for a gourmet dip if one had imbibed an hour prior to consumption.

We began the judging with the "SPAM Vegetable Frittata Delight," a casserole crammed with broccoli, green beans, corn, peas, carrots, eggs, cream cheese and Oven Roasted Turkey SPAM.

While eggs aren't my thing—I avoid eating anything in an embryonic state—this recipe really rocked, as the young folks say.

The cook, 59-year-old Rheta Merrell of Hendersonville, North Carolina, topped the casserole dish with small American flags. She said the recipe was in honor of her father, who served in the United States Army during World War II and dispensed thousands of tins of SPAM to hungry soldiers.

"It actually helped us win the war," she wrote on her entry form.

Leah and I wondered how that could be, unless the stuff had hardened up and erupted from cannons.

The SPAM contest blue ribbon went to a 7-year-old boy, Evan Lueck, who created Easy Spambled Egg Nests, a beautiful meal featuring Crescent Roll nests with a filling of SPAM, bacon, peppers (red, yellow and green), onion, shredded cheese and spices.

He arranged them like a pyramid and placed a fake (I hope) bird on top.

Here's the recipe, which is hard for me to believe was dreamed up by a 7-year-old. All those Food Network chefs better watch out. This kid is poising himself for the Iron Chef cook-offs.

Easy Spambled Egg Nests

6 eggs
¾ cup milk
1 (12 oz.) can SPAM, With Real Hormel Bacon, diced
¼ cup each of red, yellow and green bell pepper, diced
¼ cup onion, diced
8 ounces of your favorite cheese, shredded
Ground black pepper to taste

Nonstick cooking spray
2 (6-count) cans Pillsbury Big & Buttery Crescent Rolls
Additional shredded cheese (optional)
Parsley sprigs (optional)

(I never said every recipe in this book would be easy, and I probably would NEVER try this one because of all the steps, but believe me, it was a beautiful entrée.)

Step One: In three separate Ziploc bags, split the first seven ingredients equally. Carefully seal each bag and shake well.

Step Two: Bring a large pot of water to a good boil. Preheat oven to 350 degrees.

Step Three: Spray muffin pan lightly with cooking spray. Carefully stretch each triangle of Crescent Roll dough and press into each muffin cup to form a "nest."

Step Four: Place nests into the oven and bake at 350 for 15–19 minutes.

Step Five: Place all three egg bags into the pot of boiling water and turn down to a reduced boil, say, low to medium. Cook egg bags for 13–15 minutes.

Step Six: Carefully remove each bag from the boiling water and wipe with a towel. Open one bag at a time and roll the Spambled egg onto a plate and cut into four equal parts. If nests have risen too much, press with spoon while warm to enlarge the inside of the nests.

Step Seven: Spoon one part of Spambled egg mixture into its own nest. Repeat until all nests are filled. Top with additional shredded cheese and/or parsley. *Enjoy!*

For those who are SPAM inclined or curious, here are two more quick and funky recipes that won ribbons at the mountain state fair.

Cackleberry Bake
(Created by Austin Maynor, age 12)

Make this the night before and bake for breakfast.

10 to 12 slices of white bread, crusts removed
1 (12 oz.) can SPAM, drained
1¼ cup shredded cheese
6 eggs
1 cup milk
½ tsp. salt
¼ tsp. pepper

In an 8" square casserole dish, layer bread two slices deep to cover the dish.

Drain the SPAM. Then dice and fry.

Layer it on top of the bread.

Sprinkle shredded cheese over the top of the SPAM.

In a separate bowl, whisk together eggs, milk, salt and pepper. When well whisked, pour over top of bread, SPAM and cheese layers.

Cover and place in fridge overnight.

In the morning, preheat oven to 350 and bake for 25–30 minutes until light brown and bubbly.

Cowboy Caviar
(Created by Savannah Maynor, age 12)

2 (8-oz.) packages cream cheese, softened
2 bunches green onions, diced
½ cup mayonnaise (*Duke's is best, I promise*)
1 (12 oz.) can Classic SPAM, diced or processed into small pieces
2 Tbsp. fresh chives (optional)
Crackers (your choice)

Mix all ingredients until well blended and serve with crackers.

CHAPTER SEVENTEEN

Making a Mess of Collards

In the South, if you don't know how to make a "mess" of collards, you're better off not telling a soul. And if you don't know what a mess is, then you must get with the program and learn about how we grow, eat, boil—even shave—our collards and mustard greens.

This is, unless, of course, you prefer eating barely boiled kale, which is all the rage for upper-crust greens eaters and tree-huggers on a vitamin A kick.

For the real soul sister or Southern-fried chick, a mess of greens usually entails a good-sized batch of collards or mustard greens, and a seriousness about cooking them, the way the Japanese are about perfecting sushi.

In fact, we are so collard-happy, many towns bestow tiaras upon their prettiest girl and drape her in a "Collard Queen" sash, stick a scepter in her hand, put her on the flatbed of a truck and parade her fine collardy self around the square.

Being crowned "Collard Queen" is an honor, even better than being Homecoming Queen in some people's minds, because most of our collard queens are virgins, having spent their adolescence in the kitchen, while our homecoming queens are anything but, having spent their youth in the backseats of Pintos and Gremlins or on the 50-yard line at midnight after four pony Millers.

Of course, when I was LaGrange High's homecoming queen in 1978, I was a virgin for sure and remained that way for at least the two-week grace period so no one would snatch the rhinestones off my head.

Tragically, the only area in which I'm considered semivirginal these days is the kitchen. I'll confess that up until forced, I had never made a mess of collards or a mess of anything except of my very own life. I wasn't even sure which of the green things in the produce department at BI-LO WERE collards.

Anything with a stalk or head frightens me half to death, and I run from that aisle and aim my cart straight for the Tuna Helpers and frozen food section where nuking is the preferred method of cooking.

You see, I wouldn't even be in this store looking at greens had it not come my time to host the Thanksgiving meal, and the only reason I'm in charge of this multicourse dining extravaganza is that pot roast I cooked and served when I should have gone on to the hospital.

Because I didn't allow ER transport and because the meal went down without a major hitch except some tooth picking, I found myself fondling dirty greens and wishing I could renege and uninvite everyone to my little wobbly table for the Thanksgiving dinner I was guilted into preparing.

Everybody else in my family chose to up and quit cooking the Thanksgiving meal, saying it flat wore them out, and thus they began throwing more hints in my direction than common decency should allow.

" 'Bout time you did the turkey, isn't it?" Mama asked one time too many. "Everybody has to take a holiday. Once you're married and have kids, the job's gotta be divided. The torch gets passed, praise the Lord and Pillsbury biscuits."

Like most things in life, serving a big meal is in one way or another related to the goings-on of one's vag-gee-gee. Once your coochie has projectiled a kid, the meal is on you, grown girl, so get out the pot holders and the *Joy of Cooking* manual.

Being an adult in the South means having to stake out a holiday or two and volunteer the meal. As I said, once your loins have cracked open and a child's head has emerged, within two years the kin will hint or outright ask you to do the cooking—the choices being the Easter spread, Fourth of July or Labor Day cookouts, Thanksgiving, Christmas or New Year's Day—only New Year's Day doesn't really count since all you have to do is provide ham, black-eyed peas, collards (the most difficult of all dishes) and cornbread. And the Fourth of July is easy because people drink so much beer they really don't care what you serve, which in most cases is a simple meal of barbecue, Lay's chips and corn on the cob. I tried to snatch that holiday, since I could buy it all at the Squealing Pig, but too many of my kin with bad hips and backs hissed and bared teeth when I so much as suggested taking an "easy" holiday shift.

We all know the Mother of All Holiday Meals is Thanksgiving. No one really wants to do it unless she/he is a lunatic, masochist or raging sot, the latter of whom uses the big day as an excuse to tie one on.

The only way it's tolerable to cook forty-eight straight hours while having hot flashes, complicated by waves of oven heat, is for women to drink wine as they chop, kneed, degut, baste and bake. Same as for the men who decide they're going to rush out and buy the family a turkey fryer, which is no more than a crackling, greasy excuse to get knee-walking drunk and burn up the living room or front porch. Many men I know don't have eyebrows as a result. They're the ones who got off lucky. The unlucky few have lost their fiddling parts—that dangling man meat they're all so proud of and can't stop fondling.

It's my belief that nearly every sane, sober person hates to cook Thanksgiving dinner because it involves so many different dishes, including the carcass with guts, and the most massive prep time and cleanup one has ever seen. Such is why my beloved kin who secretly must hate me cornered and conned me into taking on the big *T*.

I'm thinking, "Don't you know I don't cook? Please don't let that one chuck roast I served fool you. It was a Crock-Pot roast, for heaven's sake, a one-time wonder."

This meal being passed on to me must mean the kin are desperate and will eat anything to spare them from their spatulas.

Now that I'm of age, I'll be pulling out bird innards in front of my sink this Thanksgiving and every other Thanksgiving I draw air (even if it's from an oxygen tank). I'm officially old enough to be a grandmother and yet I'm expected to do all the work and smile sweetly when someone offers to bring a pie or precooked rolls. And all the while, I'm thinking, "A pie? A bag of rolls? I'm cleaning my house for three days and all you want to bring is a pie? Why don't you chop a few vegetables and make a nice green bean casserole? Any old fool can heat up a Mrs. Smith's or a bag of Sister Schubert's."

Then I realize how mean I sound and how ungrateful for all the years I got to eat without doing so much as lifting anything heavier than a fork. This is only a rite of passage.

Not that I mind, because I love everybody. That's what Mama used to say after two cocktails in the years before she quit drinking prior to her religion and blood pressure simultaneously hitting the explosive marks. Her eyes would mist up and she'd weep and then sing in a slow, wine-lulled voice: "I just love my family. I love everybody!!! I kid you not. What a life of love I have. Thank you, Jesus. Sweet Lord of lords, I love my family to itty-bitty pieces." Boo-hoo, boo-hoo, she'd cry and commence hugging all present including the occasional stranger.

I figure the wine industry booms during the holidays not just because people get sloshed so they can tolerate their kin and those dreadful office parties, but because very few enjoy reaching like an ob-gyn into the Turk's ass region and fetching organs from dark and hollow places. It's not one's idea of a grand old time at the sink.

Yanking out frozen-solid innards is just the beginning. The housecleaning prior to guests' arrival is a whole other ball game. With my kin, you've got to get the place spotless, and with my husband's back conveniently out every November, the housework is up to me. It's not easy being both the cook and the cleaner, though I realize many a Mee-Maw can do it. I have a theory this is because they are hormone- and uterus-free, thus friendlier than the rest of us. Those with raging hormones and fickle uteruses never know what's going to transpire as they cook and serve the meal and conversation. It's a crapshoot. Give a woman in her 40s the major-league cooking gigs, and you can expect just about anything to happen.

I talked to someone the other day who's a bigwig with a local police department, and he told me about the time he went to a filthy house at Thanksgiving and took it upon himself to start vacuuming up a storm. That conversation put some fangs in my fears, and I haven't slept for days thinking about him vacuuming the hostess's house.

It doesn't help that I have the kind of kinfolk who invest in eyewear that allows them to see things not even the Hubble can spot. You take these four grandparents and give them their megastrength bifocals and they'll see every speck of dirt, stain and handprint in the joint. They'll also tell you what color underwear you're wearing.

The pressure to clean house is almost worse than that of preparing the perfect feast, because people will forgive things like an overdone turkey, but they will NOT tolerate stains on the carpet or crumbs in the kitchen. You'll be talked about as slovenly and perhaps even a no-good woman on meth or crack. The kin (particularly those belonging to you're-all-bound-for-hell churches) tend to think that if a place isn't spotless, the hostess must be spending her time in a meth lab or sleeping off Vicodin hangovers.

With all these pressures and fears swirling and clutching at my heart and threatening a string of arrhythmias such as I am prone, I had to come up with a "Surviving Thanksgiving as the Hostess" game plan, which starts with soaking the guests in wine unless they've just emerged from rehab or are chip-carrying members of a 12-step program. Typically, these teetotalers have nice manners and serenity.

Next, haul out an empty tray, preferably the good silver one, and say, "Please deposit your glasses, contacts, magnifiers and baby Hubbles right here. They shall be returned upon your departure, along with any dental wear and oral prosthetics that can't tolerate questionable cooking methods and outcomes."

If you have cats or other stinky pets such as our own personal World O' Rodents (a giant evil rabbit with huge balls and a hamster the size of a groundhog), greeting guests at the door is the perfect time to pretend you're a cologne tester at the mall and spray them thoroughly. "Georgio? Tresor? A bit of Lauren?"

Remember, these lovely people seated at your fine table ARE your own friends and relatives. When you see a trait that really gets under your skin, don't forget that very trait is likely under your own skin as well. We tend to be bothered when someone's glaring flaws mirror our own.

Here are my tried and semisuccessful tips for getting through Thanksgiving Day, first for those who are doing the cooking and next for those who are doing the guesting.

For the Cook

1. Buy either the bird (Soy Squawker or Tofu Tom) already cooked and prepared or fix it yourself. I prefer to buy the cooked bird, then, an hour before guests arrive, put it in my oven as if I've slaved all morning. Remember to defrost the thing the way it says on the package. Don't get out your blowtorches or toss the bird in the clothes

dryer, as one of my friends did from sheer desperation because she forgot to thaw two to three days ahead of time.

2. Enlist help. You've provided the house, done the cleaning, polished the silver and are risking your grandma's china for these people. So ask them to come with their arms loaded. Don't wimp out and say, "Oh, just bring yourself." That is super passive-aggressive. You tell those wonderful bums to either bring on the casserole-packed CorningWare or stay home.

3. Make most of the side dishes the night before.

4. Wake up early Thanksgiving morning, turn the parade on for the kids, and go back to bed for an extra hour of sleep so you don't have to grit your teeth and fry up nerves already on edge. The additional sleep will help more than a slew of Sutter Home.

5. When the meal is over, show those loveable bloating kinfolk your new pairs of Playtex yellow gloves. Have lots of sizes and play a game of which pair will fit whom. Then shove those hands at sponges, dishcloths, mops, and brooms, and point them toward sinks, dirty tables, floors—anywhere crumbs and dirt fester.

For the Guests

1. Bring the hostess flowers. Or if she's a boozer, bring her a nice bottle of something that will knock the edge off the hard work she's doing.

2. If you're toting children, read them the riot act before departure. One I've found effective goes like this: "All right now. Whoever acts ugly is going to get it. I will personally write Santa Claus a letter telling him you have the manners of heathens and to send all your gifts to the list of poor children at www.cherubsindireneed.com." If

that doesn't work, this will. "You want me to stuff our turkey with your i-Pod and Xbox games?"

3. Offer to clean up. Don't wait until you see the big yellow gloves coming your way.

4. Stay no more than three hours after dining unless you've been invited overnight. The hostess may have liked you at 1 PM, but by 4 or 5, she'd most likely be overjoyed to see you go.

5. Have fun. Remember what the church sign says, THANKSGIVING IS NOT JUST A HOLIDAY. IT'S AN ATTITUDE.

Best Way Turkey

Thaw it.

Clean it. *Don't forget to look inside the giant vagina thingy.*

Remove anything shaped like a baby shepherd's crook. *This would be a neck, I learned the hard way.*

Also, if it's wrapped in plastic or paper and all stuck together, you can be sure it's guts. So either toss them or chop them for gravy, if you're of that nature. *Plenty of folks like giblets (what I call gutlets) in their gravy. Not I, said the Turkey White Meat purist.*

This recipe is from an old Southern woman, probably passed along from one granny to another.

Old South Turkey

This old woman liked to cook her bird without the pretenses of today's fancier practices including frying and soaking in sea salt and/or putting the bird in enough herbs and alcohol to transform it into a laboratory experiment.

She simply cooked her turkey in an open roaster in a medium oven. First, though, she set about "mopping it well with melted butter," and as it cooked, she'd keep mopping and sopping, and would, occasionally, splash the turkey with some red wine and more butter. She found the foil wrap just as satisfactory as shoving the bird in a cooking bag.

"In my family," she said, "the stuffing has always taken precedence over the bird itself." She admits being tempted many times to skip the turkey altogether and focus on the oyster-walnut stuffing.

Oyster Walnut Stuffing

This recipe works best for a turkey in the 15-pound range.

30 slices of white bread broken into small pieces and soaked in cold water

Drain bread and sprinkle with dashes of salt, pepper, sage and vinegar.

Meanwhile, heat ½ cup butter in a heavy skillet. Add turkey giblets (finely chopped) and cook over medium heat 15–20 minutes.

Add chopped celery and two pints of oysters, drained and cleared of any shell particles.

Mix all together (add a cup of walnuts at this time), and spoon in the turkey or cook in a separate casserole until done.

CHAPTER EIGHTEEN

There's No Such Thing as a Free Bird

Don't be fooled by the grocery store banners announcing FREE TURKEYS. Believe me, nothing is free, and certainly not a 15-pound Butterball.

A coworker of mine exploded with a hissy fit at a popular supermarket when a clerk clucked about the free turkey tokens—a certain number of which would "earn" her the bird of her choice.

"FREE TURKEY!!" my friend hollered while in line at the store. "This ain't no free turkey. By my calculations this is a $600 turkey. If I come in here every Sunday and spend my weekly $100 budget, then I'm going to have to haul my butt in here six times in all to qualify. That's a $600 turkey. Nothing free about that. Why can't I qualify for two turkey tokens since I spent $100 and the requirement is $40?"

No one cracked a smile behind the registers. They noticed the giant boxes of Tampax, StayFree pads and 500-count jug of Midol next to the pigeon-sized turkey in my friend's cart.

"I was just trying to make a joke," she said, a few weeks after her trip to the frozen-turkey bin. "I didn't know they'd get in that microphone and boom out, "OVERRIDE," just to bring a manager up front. They must have found me threatening, maybe thought I was going to go psycho 'cause my free turkey was going to cost more than my living room sofa."

Not long after hearing this and knowing I was in charge of the big meal for the second consecutive year, I drove to the store to see if I couldn't rustle up some free bird. I filled the buggy with all sorts of health foods such as Little Debbie Swiss Cake Rolls and Cocoa Pebbles, and when I got to the register, the total was $42.85.

Perfect. I was due my first turkey coupon, and could all but smell the golden bird as it roasted in my mind, the spices and seasonings, the sausage and walnut stuffing filling the house with grandmotherly scents.

I envisioned the table set beautifully and the delighted relatives gazing at the most gloriously prepared turkey in history until I heard the cashier shout, "OVERRIDE on Register 7. That's an OVERRIDE on Register 7."

She glared at me as if I were a criminal.

"What is it?" I asked. "I spent over $40, didn't I?"

"You can't count your juglets of wine as part of the free-turkey program. I'm going to have to void out your total and that means you will be much too short to get a free-turkey coupon. So there."

I could see a wicked grin trying to creep up her teenaged face. This would not do, and I turned to those in line behind me to give them fair warning.

"I'm really sorry, but this may take a while. I need to run back and get twenty dollars' worth of stuff besides wine and Michelob Ultra in order to qualify for my bird token, so y'all might want to go on over to another lane."

Within ten minutes, I'd reloaded the cart with nonalcoholic items and was all but euphoric when the checkout girl handed over my turkey ticket.

"Oh, goody," I said, as she returned my VIP ELITE ADVANTAGE card. "I'll put my buggy by the service desk and run get my turkey and come back through your line, if that's OK."

She pounded a fist on the counter, some boy's chunky class ring hitting the conveyor belt. "You have to have SEVEN of these before you get the turkey!" she said.

"But I thought if—"

"Seven! Every customer must have that many. No exceptions."

"Na-Na-Ne-Boo-Boo, Beeotch," is what I murmured, slamming my cart against her counter and burning buggy rubber to bust out of there.

The next day I visited another grocery store offering a "free" turkey and ended up spending nearly a hundred dollars, earning only a single token.

"But wait," I said to the cashier. "It says here that for every $40 you spend you get the voucher. I spent over forty so I should get at least two of these free things." I remembered my coworker had encountered the same troubles.

"That's right. You spent too much. You should have divided your trip in two or three visits. It's best to come every day for seven days so you can get the required tokens for the free turkey."

FREE? Even if one spent $40 a pop, the free turkey would cost roughly $280, same as a round-trip plane ticket to New York City or for some nice Zoom! whitening at the dentist. Throw in what gas costs and that ups it to about 350 big ones.

The whole free-turkey scheme reminded me of a generous company I once worked for that pulled a corporate Grinching and snatched away our Christmas bonus checks, which equaled two weeks' pay. Instead, they decided to hand out free-turkey vouchers as a way of saying "Thank You for Pouring Your Blood and Guts into this Company, and by the way, Happy Holidays, Suckahs!"

Every single employee got a voucher worth $11.46, which may have been plenty in 1965, but as it is now, wound up being only enough to buy a partial bird unless you could find one the size of Hansi's parrot.

That same coworker who had a turkey shit fit over the grocery store free bird, clutched her "bonus" and set out fiercely determined to find a carcass at the voucher price. Red-faced and panting, she dug around in the frozen-turkey bin as if she were Dumpster diving. When she was done an hour later, she all but had frostbite on her nose and fingers.

"They put all the big ones on top," she said, "and I had to hoist them with both hands to the other section until I finally found one at the bottom of the freezer the size of a mama finch.

"It was shriveled like something Charlie Brown might get. My mother took a picture of me posing with the little wizened turkeyette," she said, laughing hysterically and mocking her company's generosity.

For a while, she even saved the turkey voucher, thinking she might glue it around a Christmas ball for a memorable ornament, a testament to the joys of corporate America's giving spirit.

Not to be outdone or daunted, I finally collected enough grocery store coupons for a "free turkey"—seven trips to the store that set me back roughly $450.

It would have cost $15.29 without the coupons, so do the math. Had I known turkeys that year were going to be cheaper than Alpo, I wouldn't have entered the free-bird race.

Regardless, I couldn't resist anything "free" and we loaded up with a big frozen bird, which was probably going to be tough and dry—one of those second-rate turkeys you wish you had an extra row of teeth to gnaw through.

I'd most likely have to tell that same old lie as I witnessed kinfolk losing crowns and partials, and searching through the dressing for fillings and implants.

"It's a Butterball," I'd say, hiding the bag stamped in huge black letters: GENERIC CORPORATE COUPON TURKEY OF UN-KNOWN GENDER AND ORIGIN.

My mother-in-law, the expert on Butterball turkeys and expensive hams, would no doubt give me a look that said, "You lying little thing."

"It ended up being about $500," I'd announce with great pride. "Most expensive turkey money can buy." Then I'd grin. "Bon Appétit."

One tradition I've started every year—besides (accidentally) leaving in the innards as the bird festers at Bake 350—is quizzing young kids about cooking a turkey, starting with my daughter right after we'd read our Junie B. Jones book for the night.

"So," I said. "How do you think a person cooks a turkey?"

She opened her sleepy brown eyes and gave them a classic Junie B. Jones roll.

"Mom," she said. "First you have to take the particles out. Remember you left the heart in last year 'cause it fell out of the turkey's fanny and everybody got all grossed out?"

"Well, anyone could have made that mistake. In some cultures and on *Fear Factor*, hearts are a delicacy."

"I'd go ahead and take the slimy stuff out," she said. "You're supposed to make room to stuff it with corn and carrots, maybe some peas and dog pooh," she said, laughing and twisting around in the bed. "You can also stuff it with Kleenexes and baby diapers and boys' stinky underpants."

OK. She was at that point where sleep should have arrived an hour earlier, that delirious, silly phase at night when kids make you laugh the most. It's almost as if they get surges of creativity right before they nod off to sleep.

"Don't forget to cut off its head," she said. "If you don't have enough inside that big hole already, you can stuff it with dirty socks and panty hose and then say, 'Oh, pooey. Let's go to Nana's to eat Thanksgiving dinner.'"

I decided to poll a couple of the neighborhood children on the subject.

"Tell me, how would you cook a turkey?" I asked Ariel Monteith, a delightful 9-year-old who lives down the street.

"OK," she said, her voice getting all serious. "You bake it

for an hour at about 5 degrees. It goes in a pan, and I'm going to stuff mine with candy corn and whipped cream. I may put some gravy on it."

Tiffany, another little girl down the road, firmly believes a person goes to "Little Pigs BBQ" to get a turkey. She must be confusing her farm animals.

"You take it home," she said, "and put a scarf around it that you'll cook it in. It's called a cooking scarf. When you put the scarf on, it will get hot and burst into flames. And everyone will eat it up."

My own daughter, about 7 at the time, had a final thought before drifting off to sleep.

"I know what else you stuff a turkey with," she said all sweetly.

"What?" I asked.

"Love," she cooed. "Pure love."

Scrawny Corporate-Voucher Turkey

Put runt turkeys given by corporate America in a Crock-Pot along with lots of potatoes and carrots. Season with a heavy hand.

Because the shriveled bird won't feed more than two or three, it's best to get a turkey breast and roast it on the side.

Place a sign on the runt turkey: COMPLIMENTS OF TWENTY YEARS OF SERVICE TO THE MAN.

CHAPTER NINETEEN

My Alcoholic Cat

Daddy always said if it wasn't for alcoholic beverages, our economy might sink and most meals wouldn't get eaten. It appears when a man purchases high-ticket items, it's much easier on him if two beers are under his belt, thus loosening his wallet.

He never knew that one day a drunken cat would be directly responsible for one of the biggest purchases of his life.

It all started when Mama quit drinking and my sister adopted an alcoholic cat. My mama knows not to bother Daddy until happy hour has loosened his belt and inhibitions.

She used to drink with him, but then she found Jesus and a few Bible verses at almost the exact same time her doctor found high blood pressure and a few benign lumps beneath her skin. She decided to forgo that mellow feeling of being in the middle of one's second drink just as a warm sun is descending and life's sharp edges seem sandpapered and smoothed.

The cat took her place.

Samantha, who looked as if she spawned from a landfill, was an alcoholic from the time she was about six weeks old, having been raised in a frat house at the University of Georgia where she awakened daily to feed upon fried chicken and mashed potato scraps along with keg beer. On special occasions she got Margaritas or whatever concoction the frat guys had brewed up to seduce the sorority girls during mixers.

We inherited Sam because my younger sibling was a Little Sister at the frat house. In the Greek system, fraternities choose girls they like or want to boink and invite them to join the Little Sister roster.

At the end of college, Sister Sandy packed up all her belongings and waited on Daddy to drive up in his silver pimp-mobile Cadillac with the U-Haul attached to the back.

She slid into the passenger seat, Samantha struggling and hissing in her arms.

"You're not bringing a cat home, young lady," Daddy said, eyeing the scraggly, bleary-eyed creature. "That thing looks rabid."

"We can get it some shots," Sandy said. "It'll be left to die if—"

"Your mama already has two cats and isn't about to take one on that looks like death warmed over. Now, run on back up to that big house and give it to one of those boys sitting by that keg on the porch."

Sandy hugged the cat close to her body. It attacked and behaved like a wild rabbit. "I can't," she said. "No one will take her but me."

"You're not going to be her saving—"

"Please, Daddy. I'll take care of her and as soon as I get a job, it'll go off into the real world with me. Y'all won't have her but a few weeks, I'm sure."

Daddy has never been one to refuse my sister much. She has huge brown moose eyes and a pout like a supermodel's. She's tiny and butterfly-like in her movements, a graceful girl much unlike me. Whereas I chose to go into print media, she chose television for all the world to see and hear her charms.

My daddy saw the tears that sprang to Sandy's eyes and are typically accompanied by her famous lip quiver. "Just a few weeks?" he asked, staring at his daughter and the wild cat.

"Thank you, thank you, thank you. I love you, Daddy. You're the best."

The drive from Athens, Georgia, to Spartanburg, South Carolina, was about two and a half hours. The cat moaned and howled, whined and emitted guttural sounds, as if it were about to give birth or die on the spot. Daddy would glance over and see it trembling and fretting; an animal that seemed ready to jump straight out of its own fur.

"What's wrong with that cat?" he asked, turning into a gas station just outside of Commerce, Georgia.

Sandy drew a deep breath and stared at Daddy for a minute. "I forgot to tell you this one little thing." She scrunched up her cute little future-anchorwoman face. "Sam's an alcoholic. We just need to get her a beer or two and—"

"Hey, now. Whoa. What did you say about this little waif of a cat?"

"She drinks. And not like a lady. More like a two-fisted frat boy." Sandy couldn't help but laugh. Daddy couldn't help but cease respirations.

"Just go in," my sister said, "and get her an Old Milwaukee or any other cheap beer."

My father seemed zombied, as if zapped with a tranquilizer gun. Sandy shook his shoulder. "Dad? A beer? It'll fix everything. You'll see. Look, I have Sam's saucer right here."

Dad got out of the long silver Cadillac and lifted the gas nozzle to fill the tank with midgrade. The sun bore on his graying hair and closed eyes. After a few minutes, the nozzle clicked and he put the hose back into place.

Sandy rolled down the window. "Beer? Please?"

Daddy walked into the convenience store and was gone quite some time. When he returned, he carried a brown paper sack, the exact shape of a six-pack.

"It's Bud Lite," he said, easing into the car. "You reckon she'll like it?"

"She's not picky. Once we get it in her, she'll quit shaking and start acting more like a nice kitty with dignity and manners."

My dad sort of shook his head. He's used to kooks in the family, having married a woman who has a wild sister, our Aunt Betty—the one who owned and harbored a pet skunk and who at 70 likes to do gymnastics and cut flips in front of the preacher and anyone else who'll watch her land a perfect split. Aunt Betty paved the way, so we owe her a debt of gratitude.

Sandy opened the sack and pulled the tab on a beer, pouring it into the yellow saucer that once served as an ashtray. "Don't worry, darling boo," she cooed to the cat. "We're gonna fix you right up. You'll be good as new in no time."

My dad watched the entire bartending scene with interest and concern. This act of partaking in alcohol while in a vehicle came long before the Open Container law, so in a way, it was legal for a cat to booze it up while someone else was driving.

Even before Sandy could lower the saucer the cat was standing on her hind legs, ready to get at the beer.

"Lord," Daddy said. "That's a shame, isn't it?"

Samantha slurped as if she hadn't had fluids in a week. She didn't pause until the saucer was dry. "Those PETA people find out about this and they'll come after you," he told my sister, who was petting Sam and telling her, "Your nerves should be fine now, sweet baby kitty love. It's OK, Sammy Pooh."

"What happened to her fur?" Daddy asked. "What happened to her left ear? It's torn in half."

Sandy tipped the can of Bud Lite and refilled the cat's saucer. "Fighting. She fights like a Pit Bull, but not when she's buzzing. When she gets a good buzz, she's so gentle. See? Look at this baby love."

Daddy drove along the interstate and every now and then would toss his peripheral vision at the cat. He'd never seen such a mess and was wondering what our mother was going to do when he brought home this wreck of a drunken animal.

The thing didn't want to stop drinking and continued until every bit of beer had been drained from the second round.

"Don't give that cat another drop," he ordered. "I'm not going to be responsible for you killing the thing before we get home."

Sandy picked up the cat, now limp and purring, and held her up for Dad's inspection.

"Geez, this ain't right," Dad said. He's college educated, but like many Southerners upon viewing something abnormal and shocking, will revert to the vernacular. "I ain't supporting this habit every day."

"You'll regret it if you don't," Sandy said. "She's very mean and unpredictable if she doesn't get beer. Or wine. You can give her some of your jug wine and she'll be fine with that. She's a cheap drunk, doesn't even need a cork."

"Funny. You're some kind of funny. Wait until your mama gets a load of that sot."

By the time they got home, the cat had awakened from the gauzy sleep of booze. She was not happy, but feisty and growling, trying to scratch my father and sister and arching her back in hisses.

"We better tank her up before your mama sees her," Dad said, becoming complicit in the act of bathing a cat in adult beverages. They gave the cat a snoot full and went inside.

My mother, being devout in her faith and service, accepted the cat and her flaws and was happy my father once again had someone to drink with come 5 o'clock every day.

The two would grab a couple of beers or a jug of wine and climb the stepladder to the roof of the house where they could watch the sun sink into the white pines, oaks and maples while they sipped and lapped up their spirits.

One day during their happy hour, the phone rang.

Mama picked it up.

"Do what?" she asked. A telemarketer was on the other end.

"I said it's two-for-one and we'll never have another special like this one. It's now or never," the slick salesman said.

Oh, why had Mama agreed to be in the church directory? Every hawker in town had been calling.

"Well, you know . . . If you call back in an hour, my husband and the cat will be lit up enough that he, my husband, that is, might just buy something from you."

When the hopeful salesman called back, sure enough, Daddy was prime bait and agreed that, "Yes, it would be more preferable to be laid to rest in a mausoleum with heating and air-conditioning, with carpet and restroom facilities, than buried in the cold wet, wormy earth."

That little happy hour with the cat ended up costing around ten grand.

"We put it all on VISA," Mama said, "and guess what?"

"What?" I couldn't have prepared myself for what she said next.

"We earned enough frequent flyer miles to go to Spain. You'll have to babysit the cat. Isn't that great? You buy your burial bed and end up with a paid vacation!"

Pet Hors d'Oeuvres

1 bottle Gallo Merlot (has a convenient twist-off cap)
1 six-pack Old Milwaukee or other cheap beer
1 box Cheez-Its (or if it's a particularly beautiful sunset, RITZ with cheddar slices)

If you're inclined to enjoy some romance after climbing down off the roof, put the cat aside and grill this sensuous feast that takes no more than two brain cells to prepare and three or four ingredients on the shelf. This recipe is courtesy of Nancy Twigg, a sexy member of the Read It Or Not, Here We Come Book Club of which I'm a longtime member in poor standing because I don't read every book and always bring crappy appetizers.

Nancy is NOT a kitchen virgin. She's a kitchen SLUT—in that she can cook anything and everything and make it taste like a 5-star restaurant's head chef prepared it.

*None of her pets has ever had trouble with booze or entered detox.

Nancy's London Broil

Buy a tender and small piece of London Broil.

Marinate for an hour *(as soon as you get off work, out of jail, etc.)*.

Sprinkle on some Worcestershire sauce, olive oil, cracked black pepper and spices of choice. Never use salt. *Dries out the meat, Nancy says.*

Grill. With an electric knife slice on the diagonal. *Serve with plenty of Greek salad and dressing.*

A dish of Cherry Garcia frozen yogurt is a nice way to end the meal.

CHAPTER TWENTY

If the Sushi Isn't Fried, Pass the Boiled Peanuts

I have a really good friend named Rhett—yes, he was named after the honorable Rhett Butler—just as many a Southern girl is called Scarlett. If you haven't noticed, most Scarletts turn out to be slutty and most Rhetts, conceited. This is a generalization, and if you have a child named either of these *Gone With the Wind* monikers, good for you. I'm sure they are on the honor roll and volunteer at homeless shelters.

My friend Rhett is a real Southern gentleman and big-time connoisseur of good old trashy eating. This would include Little Debbies, boiled peanuts, anything Cajun, anything dropped in a deep fryer, and anything with questionable origins and ingredients. He cut his teeth on Cheese Puffs and Vienna sausages, pronounced in these parts "Vi-eee-ners."

When Rhett decides to cook, which is often and includes alcoholic beverages while he grills and blackens a variety of carcasses, he frequently brings me the results. Also, when he makes a meal, he invariably burns parts of his body on flames from the grill or stove. Drinking and flammables equal scorched skin and lack of body hair.

Rhett regularly appears at the Y with singed eyebrows and tales of second-degree burns on parts of his body I've never even known existed on men. Let me say one thing for the record: I won't ever be able to face a man again if he utters the most awful word in the male anatomical dictionary to me—and that word is "scrotum." Never in the history of the English language has there been a grosser-sounding word.

"Were you drinking and cooking?" I asked, staring at the crispy hairs that were once his dark, sultry eyebrows.

"Drinking? No, fool. Well, OK, I'd had four, but spaced them out over a whole hour."

"You're the fool. The body can't process but one alcoholic drink per hour. Not four!"

I love Rhett because he is so trusting he believes everything you tell him. We were in the weight room one afternoon at the Y (before I decided exercising wasn't worth the trouble of finding a parking place), and he said, "What are y'all having for dinner tonight?"

I gave it some thought and decided to pull one over on him. "Well, now," I mused. "We're having a wonderful new dish from the Asiatic Sea called 'Pussafish.'"

I wish you could have seen his face. "What'd you say?"

"It's on sale at Ingles and is the flakiest, most delicious fish you can buy. Actually, this is the first time ever you can get it in the United States. Didn't you see that huge article on it? It was taboo for years due to an issue with near-extinction." Rhett moved from the deltoid machine to the stomach cruncher, and I followed. "What happened is, the scientists urged the fish to fornicate and now we've got it over here to enjoy."

He seemed completely lost and gave up on his crunches. "What did you call that fish, again? The name of it?"

Oh, I had him now. "Pussafish," I said, trying hard not to laugh. "It's unbelievable. They have it for $7.99 a pound at Ingles's Seafood Market. Tell Sarge I sent you, and he'll give you the freshest and flakiest of all his Pussafish stock."

The next day Rhett went to work and asked all the girls in his office if they'd ever eaten Pussafish.

"You're a pervert," one said. "I'm taking your ass to HR."

(Human Resources: that place you enter and never return gainfully employed.)

"No, I'm serious, Rhett," I said when he called from work to say his female coworkers weren't too happy about the name of this fish. "We went to Ingles last night after a friend swore it was a brand-new fish just made available in the U.S. I asked the man if he had some Pussafish on hand, and he told me he was fresh out. He said, 'Woman, I've had more Pussafish in my time than most men. My testosterone tested out the roof.' "

"The women told me you were pulling my leg. Tell the truth, Susan. There's really no such thing as a Pussafish, is there?"

I laughed so hard I didn't need an ab-crunching machine. He slammed down the phone.

A week later, the girls in his office decided to play a mean old trick on him because he's gullible and too nice for his own good. They put him in the passenger side of their Honda Accord and took him out for sushi.

Rhett is an Alabama native whose knowledge of good eatin' includes bream, crappie, catfish and other wigglies pulled from brackish lake water with rusty hooks hanging from cane poles. He is a fool for the Crimson Tide and anything with an Alabama logo. If there was sushi called "Roll Tide," he'd eat every last one, no matter he has a motto that if it isn't grilled or fried, it doesn't enter his stomach.

Sushi goes against all the rules of Southern fish eating. Mainly because it's raw. We don't abide by raw. We like our steaks done and our chicken fried. We love cornmeal coating on our fish, prior to dropping it in a deep fryer filled with oil. If we feel we need to eat healthfully, we'll sub out the Crisco and use Canola instead.

Rhett couldn't understand why his female coworkers would demand he visit the Asian eatery and load him up with rice rolled in seaweed and topped in ocean creatures, some of which had suckers and tentacles and one, he later swore, that had pleading, soulful eyes staring up from the little spiral on which it lay.

A real man, Rhett said, would never eat a squid or sliver of uncooked salmon. That's for sissies and idiots who are trying hard to lure worms so they can lose weight or skip out of work and get some disability to fund their Vicodin 'scripts and fill their crack pipes.

Being a triple Southerner—that is a girl who's lived in Georgia and both the Carolinas—my initial thoughts about sushi weren't promising and bordered along the lines of Rhett's thinking.

While I'd always believed you could eat anything if it was battered beyond recognition and fried in Wesson oil or lots of butter, I wasn't sure about raw fish wrapped in rice and seaweed.

It reminded me of the days my daddy and his Schlitz-drinking buddies would pay me a quarter if I ate raw oysters.

To its credit, sushi, at least, is beautiful and artistic as well as glamorous-sounding. All the movie stars and models rave about sushi and usually rush for the nearest sushi bar as soon as they get out of rehab.

I recently signed up for a hot Kundalini yoga class in downtown Asheville (where the hippies and cool congregate) and Andie MacDowell, the movie star, is one of the students and goes for sushi many nights after sweating two buckets. It's just so . . . so . . . hip.

What else would one eat after intense yoga or chanting? "Hey, wanna grab a sack of Krystal burgers?" That dinner bell doesn't ring, now, does it?

Other people—the non–movie stars or praying mantis–sized models—who get all enraptured over these pin(worm)wheels of "health" seem to have thin thighs and lots of education. They don't talk like hicks or have bumper stickers that say, IF IT AIN'T PRIED FROM ASPHALT, IT AIN'T WORTH EATIN'.

Sushi (prior to Atkins fever) used to be the only thing the

skeleton crowds would put near their lips besides espresso and Marlboro Lights.

Because Asheville is a town that considers itself cool and cultured, diverse and perverse, it was only a matter of time that we could boast as many sushi bars as Baptist churches.

Trying to branch out from my usual Arby's Market Fresh sandwich with curly fries, I decided to become a sushi eater, thus upping my sophistication level and canceling out the fact I've eaten twenty-seven SPAM recipes and love uncooked Ramen noodles.

"Can you get sushi fried?" I remember asking years ago, back in the early nineties when one poll showed only 12 percent of Southerners like sushi. I'd watch Yankees and Californians gulp it down with a layer of ginger and wasabi, maybe a hint of soy sauce, and not even wince, though their eyes blazed and noses dripped onto their plates.

This whole sushi thing was bound to strike Rhett sooner or later. He's somewhat of a celebrity because he hosts a local TV show, and his entire body for months once graced the side of our city buses while he posed eating a giant hamburger. His usual lunch place, where he's a die-hard regular, is Fuddruckers, which boasts the best hamburgers in the world.

He begged his coworkers to take him to Fudds or the "cornbread" place, but instead they pulled into the sushi bar and forced Rhett to load up his plate.

He pouted (he is prone to histrionics), but was so hungry he figured he could eat a raw eel and squid parts if given enough ketchup and salt. He badly wanted to order a 22-ounce Bud Lite but had to go back to work.

When the meal was over, he didn't have a lot of positive things to say about sushi or its accompanying sauces.

He called me on the phone pretending to be close to tears. "They serve forms of 'food' that could also be considered as bait," said poor Rhett who swore he'd never let another woman fool him in his life. "At least I tried it. I tried it and I don't like it. Our motto in Alabama is 'We don't eat it if it didn't come off a highway or grill.' "

He told me that his lady friends suggested he might enjoy the sushi better if he decorated it with some lovely green wasabi. Rhett, poor boy, had no idea what wasabi was.

"It looked like Play-Doh," he said. "They made me eat that green glob of goo. It was hot, and I mean hot. It burnt the hairs out of my nose and they fell off into my rice like elongated pepper."

After lunch, a still-starving Rhett decided to get even with his coworkers for taking him to what he referred to as the "docks" for lunch.

"I grabbed a dead fish out of our accountant's tank," he said. "Conveniently, it had just croaked."

Rhett stuffed the fish into the air-conditioning vent in a coworker's office. Later that day, he went to Starbucks. Everyone was ordering cappuccinos and lattes and drinks he couldn't pronounce, including espresso, which hicks call "Express-O."

"What will you have, sir?" the caffeine specialist asked.

Rhett thought about this carefully, and in his hot-buttered 'Bama accent, he said, "Cawfee. Plain."

That afternoon, his belly still recoiling, Rhett knew he had to placate his stomach or it would turn on him. He couldn't make peace with his innards, knowing they'd digested a meal of raw fish and seaweed, so he did what every good Southern boy named Rhett or otherwise would do. He found him a place that sold boiled peanuts, regular and Cajun. He bought a pound of each and began peeling and sucking the salty, slimy nuts and juices from their wet paper sacks.

He knows, as many of us do, nothing hits the spot like boiled peanuts, pronounced "boy-illed" or "bald," and a delicacy many don't appreciate probably because people of questionable reputation typically sell them roadside.

Sometimes, you can even buy them in a gas station where they simmer in Crock-Pots for customers who, after filling up with unleaded, decide to fill up on boiled peanuts. They are cheap and satisfying, much like a salt lick on the rim of a Margarita glass. Haven't you ever seen people licking away at their Margarita glasses? Must be some sort of deficiency.

The problem most people have with boiled peanuts is the texture. It's eerily similar to boiled okra. The slime factor doesn't win favors, especially among Yankees and other non-Dixied folks. For those of us who love boiled peanuts, it's that slime that's so sublime, otherwise we'd eat them raw or roasted.

Once, when Mama and I took the kids to the Redneck Riviera (Myrtle Beach) we had to stop six times during our vacation for boiled peanuts sold at the various roadside markets, bubbling cauldrons stirred by men with gaping dark holes for smiles. I'm not sure what makes us crave them, but we do, and when we see a sign advertising FRESH BOILED PEANUTS, we scream and stomp the floorboard until the driver pulls over.

"If you don't stop, I'm jumping out of the car," my sister once threatened our father, who believes that from the moment a trip hath begun it should under no circumstances be interrupted. He was elated the year he discovered Tupperware wasn't just excellent for keeping raw oysters fresh but also proved an exceptional slop jar (urinal) as well.

"You people with cricket bladders can use this round dish," he'd say. "It's almost the size of a regular crapper."

We aren't the only family insane for boiled peanuts. According to an expert named Linda Stradley and her article on the Web site "What's Cooking America," boiled peanuts are a traditional snack in South Carolina, North Carolina, Georgia, northern Florida, Alabama and Mississippi.

"They are an acquired taste," she writes, "but according to Southerners, they are totally addictive. From May through November, all over the South, you will see roadside stands—ranging from woodsheds to shiny trailers—offering fresh boiled peanuts. One of the more traditional ways to eat them is to drop the shelled nuts into a bottle of RC Cola and take a swig."

Here are a few facts you may not know about boiled peanuts that Stradley uncovered in her research:

"One starts out with green or raw nuts that are boiled in salty water for hours outdoors over a fire. The shells turn soggy, and the peanuts take on a fresh legume flavor. A green peanut is not green in color, just freshly harvested. It takes ninety to a hundred days to grow peanuts for boiling, and they are available only during the aforementioned months (May through November) throughout the Southern states. One of the drawbacks of boiled peanuts is that they have a very short shelf life unless refrigerated or frozen. If you leave them out on the kitchen counter for three to four days, they become slimy and smelly."

Sounds like sushi to me. Or a fish in someone's air-conditioning vent.

"No one knows just why Southerners started boiling peanuts or who was the first to boil them," Stradley writes. "However, it is known that boiled peanuts have been a Southern institution since at least the Civil War (1861–1865), when Union General William T. Sherman led his troops on their march through Georgia. As a result of General Sherman's campaign in Georgia, the Confederacy was split in two and deprived of much-needed supplies."

Because meats were scarce, the soldiers looked elsewhere for their protein and discovered boiled peanuts.

Stradley wrote that, "On May 1, 2006, Gov. Mark Sanford came to York County and officially signed into law, H.4585, to make the boiled peanut the official state snack food. Tom Stanford, a Winthrop University graduate, came up with the idea in a government class because he likes boiled peanuts."

Much can be learned about people from a simple bag of these things. I once had the privilege of eating lunch with four wonderful women I'd never met in my life. When you're a local newspaper columnist who writes about personal things, people tend to think they know you and invite you to lunch. If it's women, I usually go, and this was a great group. It was as if we'd grown up together.

The laughter among the women was as healing as any phar-
maceutical. Such is why we gals have our book clubs, bridge
clubs, Red Hat Societies and any old excuse to get together
and act anything but our age.

While sharing a meal with these women, one of whom was
Sylvia Platt, mother of TEN children and originally from
Long Island, I was reminded that Asheville proper is becoming
less and less, well . . . Southern.

I was the only woman with a drawl/twang combination, and
the only one who had eaten and adored boiled peanuts. I was
also reminded that when it comes to Southern foods, most of
my precious Yankee friends have only tasted grits. And they
hate them.

When dear Rhett returned green about the face from his
sushi lunch, he brought me two sacks of boiled peanuts—pure
heaven. It turns out, after mentioning boiled peanuts to the group
of four ladies at lunch, only one had tried them, and she hated
the taste and texture.

With that I decided to do a taste test among office workers
and friends who had planted their fannies here from other
parts of the world, places where boiled peanuts served by
weathered geezers on the roadside aren't part of the culture.

Diane Robinson, a no-nonsense blonde who used to work
our front counter and professionally greeted customers, warily
agreed to try a boiled peanut one Friday. I've noticed people
are much more willing to do things on Fridays they wouldn't
dare do on Mondays. I believe it's because they are already an-
ticipating the adult beverages soon to slow down their brains.

She picked up a dripping nut and asked, "Why are they
dark brown?"

"Because they're boiled," I said.

"What's bald?"

"Boy-illed."

"I think I'll pass," she said and went back to work. "Maybe
another day, another year. Maybe if we have a famine."

Later that afternoon at work, on a dark chocolate and Goody Powder high, I toted my peanuts around to every Northerner I could locate.

Diane finally agreed—she was famished—and at last tasted them. "They're too soft," she said. "Aren't peanuts supposed to be firm?" Her face said it all and I knew not to offer her seconds. She crouched under her desk and spit into the trash can. Next I tried them on my dear friend Dorothy, who may be from Michigan but eats collards and has a bit of a Southern accent.

She grabbed a few. "How do you eat these?" she asked. "I'll show you." I cracked one as the juices ran down my forearms and quickly opened my mouth to slurp it all up.

Dorothy is a great sport and sucked one down without making a face. Then, to my surprise, she asked for another.

"I like them," she said, reminding me of the book *Green Eggs and Ham.* "I really do."

Just as she was glowing about them, a Tennessee native walked by and nearly gagged. "I hate those things," she said, the blasphemous words an assault. "I despise them and anyone who eats them."

"But you're from Tennessee," I protested.

"That doesn't mean I have no taste."

In the end, I guess boiled peanuts, along with sushi, are kind of like politicians. You either like them, preferably with a lot of beer, or you never want to see them in your life.

Here is a recipe for Boiled Peanuts.

Boiled Peanuts
(From COOKS.COM Recipe Search)

Bring a large pot (about 7 quarts) of water to a boil.

Pour in ¼ cup of salt (canning or kosher salt is less exprensive).

Drop peanuts into boil; put a plate on top of peanuts.

Fill a jar with water and set on top of plate to keep peanuts under the water.

Cook over high heat until peanuts begin to boil.

Turn off heat.

Allow to cool.

When cool, bring to a boil again and cook for about 15 minutes.

CHAPTER TWENTY-ONE

Kitchen Virgins and Kitchen Trollops

My friend Margie admits to something most Southern women would die before acknowledging. She openly confessed that she farted. And not just alone but in the company of a brand-new fellow.

"I tooted like crazy all day," she said of a date following a cooking disaster that had her stomach and intestines churning and twisting. "It was our first real get-together, too."

Margie said it all started in 1999 when, after getting over the breakup of a ten-year relationship, she decided to make a bold move and look for love on the Internet.

"My good friend met her future husband this way and she was very up on this method as a new way to meet men."

Margie joined a chat room called "40-Plus and Sexy, Too." She met a great man named Jim who was an accountant for the Social Security Administration and about five years her senior. He was from a small town in Georgia, a graduate of Auburn University and a huge college football fan, just like Margie.

"After chatting online and on the phone for about two months, we decided to meet in Tallahassee about halfway between Orlando (where I lived at the time) and Atlanta. We both drove up for the day only, and experienced lust at first sight, and I arranged for him to come to Orlando the next weekend."

They enjoyed the football game, watching the Florida State University Seminoles, and getting all worked up over each other as well.

Then the trouble started, as it will when food and lust don't mix and stomachs roil.

"I decided to do something fun and have rib eye steaks on the grill, my special Italian potato salad (recipe to follow), baked beans, corn on the cob and sliced tomatoes. After all, at 6'5", Jim liked a good-sized meal."

The evening went beautifully and the food proved delicious. The next morning, they got up and ate cereal with bananas and granola and then hit the road to St. Petersburg for a gun show, as Jim collected antique rifles.

"Being in Florida, it was as hot as can be so we had the windows rolled up and the AC on," Margie said. "Somewhere about an hour into the three-hour trip, my stomach erupted. Baked beans, corn, bananas, granola . . . I will leave it to your imagination the aroma in that car."

Margie said they struggled with the windows rolled down to make it all the way to St. Petersburg.

"My constant apologies (about tooting) finally caused him to break down in hysterical laughter," she said. "The trip home was just as bad. The Tums I'd bought and gorged on didn't help at all."

Once she made it back to her house, Margie locked herself in the bedroom and cringed while he watched the Saturday night football games. The next day, she drove him to the airport.

"Big surprise," she said. "I never saw him again."

She swears this was her choice, but I've always heard farting and bathroom talk leads to the Death of Romance. I once had a date who die-reared in our guest bathroom and I never spoke to him again. Ever heard of the flush lever, dude?

Margie said she did learn a valuable lesson. A 40-plus woman has no business eating when she wants to be sexy. Too much can go awry in the digestive process.

Italian Potato Salad

Serves 12

1 5-pound bag redskin potatoes, with skin left on and cut into quarters
1 cup chopped celery
1 cup chopped onions
1 cup sliced black olives
10 bacon strips, cooked very crisp and drained until dry, with drippings preserved
1 jar good Italian salad dressing
1 cup mayonnaise
Salt and pepper to taste

Cook potatoes until soft.
Drain and chill for one hour, and cut into quarters.
Once chilled, in a large Tupperware bowl, add the next four ingredients and mix well.
Crumble the bacon and add it and the bacon drippings.
Add the salad dressing, the mayonnaise, and salt and pepper.
Mix well. Chill for 2 hours before serving.

Joyce Dover (the Possum Roast lady,) is by all means an exceptional cook. Yet even the pros run into trouble every now and then. Seems a few Cornish hens got the best of her one afternoon when she grew bold and decided, even though she'd never tried them, she'd cook a few for dinner.

"I didn't figure I needed a cookbook," she said, concerning

these little game hens. "What could you do with something so small other than cook it until it's done and salt and pepper it a little?"

Joyce stuck the hens in the microwave after washing them carefully and laying them on a plate.

"I turned the microwave on, thinking about thirty minutes should cook it tender," she said. "I went on about my kitchen duties, then all of a sudden, I heard a loud POOF and perhaps a quaint little chirp. I looked into the microwave glass door and saw the little birds had been heaved into the air by force, turned over and landed back in the plate."

Joyce opened the door, and all that remained, she said, were the skeletons.

"Where the meat went, I don't have a clue. It's the last time I've ever blown up Cornish game hens and the last time I attempted to cook one."

OTHER KITCHEN DISASTERS

DC Stanfa, author of *The Art of Table Dancing: Escapades of an Irreverent Woman*, is the only friend I've ever had whose exploits got her booked on *Jerry Springer*—a woman who, in a long formal gown, "gatored" at a highfalutin author's ball filled with best-selling writers.

Here's her story in her own words. Let's call it a disaster, with a quick save at meal's end.

Murphy's Slaw
by DC Stanfa

It was a mixed marriage and doomed to failure. He is from the South, and I am of Northern descent. The clash of cultures came early, while we were dating. He took me to North Carolina to meet his parents. It wasn't exactly a reenactment of

Green Acres, but when city and country collide—especially in the kitchen—watch out for the cutlery.

Mom and Pop were good small-town Southerners who are suspicious of anyone who isn't direct kin or doesn't go to the same church. (I don't mean of the same religion, as in Lutheran, I am referring to the actual building they worship in, just down the road from their house. Coincidentally, most of the church members are kin to them as well.) Being a Yankee, an older woman and a baptized Catholic were already three strikes against me. I was hypothetically out before ever going to bat as potential daughter-in-law material. God forbid they found out I owned a microwave and listened to music by "The Other Elvis," as in Costello.

From the moment I set foot in the house, I did my best to fit in. This meant hanging out in the kitchen, where God intended women to be, while the menfolk watched football on TV.

Three activities officially took place in the kitchen: cooking, eating and cleaning up. The men visited the kitchen briefly to plow through the eating portions and grab strong beverages, while the women spent the entire day in this room engaging in all the scullery work, plus another unofficial "duty" of sizing up the new Yankee woman.

I, of course, promptly offered to help with food preparation. Little did these women know that I'd been making entire meals since high school. (It is here I will interject to say DC is a KITCHEN HO.)

I could whip up some yummies, ranging from bacon-wrapped water chestnuts, to homemade spaghetti sauce, to cheesecake. Due to my questionable upbringing and uncertain (to them) cooking abilities, however, I was given a task they probably deemed simplest and least likely for me to screw up. Smug as I was, panic as big as the buckle on the Bible Belt hit me when they asked me to make the coleslaw.

Sure, I'd eaten plenty of coleslaw in my life. At places like

KFC and Catholic Friday-night fish fries, that is. Coleslaw was not a staple in the Stanfa household, nor in any of my friends' homes, up north in Ohio. Salad was our side dish of choice. We ate the heck out of salads.

While I had visions of iceberg, spinach, romaine and radicchio dancing through my head, someone handed me a head of cabbage. I looked at them as if they'd offered me the head of the Queen of France. Horror and terror flashed like neon signs on my face.

"You DO know how to make coleslaw?" said my now not-likely-to-be-sister-in-law.

I stared down at the Cabbage Head Queen, hoping it would whisper a clue. It wasn't talking. "Let them eat cake. Lettuce eat salad." I imagined the Queen placing food orders and saving me from the shame of my sin.

After what seemed like hours of internal deliberation and hundreds of disapproving eyes, I placed the cabbage on the counter, signaling both defeat and surrender. Mom-in-law-maybe was quick to forgive, take pity and rescue my non-Southern soul from the depths of food-failure hell. She opened a jar of mayonnaise, grabbed a cup of sugar, handed me a shredder and a bowl, and instructed me to simply shred the cabbage. Nothing more was said, although a bewildered aunt left the room, likely off to share my inadequacies with the menfolk stationed in front of the TV.

Perhaps I'm a masochist, or maybe I just can't leave not-so-well enough alone. The next day, Boyfriend and I went to the grocery store. I surprised the family that evening with my famous bacon-wrapped water chestnuts—a delicacy they'd never even heard of. Although I soon discovered that they never ate before a meal—"appetizer" didn't appear to be part of their vocabulary—the dish was devoured during dinner.

And watching Aunt Bewilderment pop a third piece in her mouth, I knew my kitchen redemption was sweeter than the slaw.

DC's Bacon-Wrapped Water Chestnuts

This appetizer can be made ahead, refrigerated and then heated up in a microwave.

1 pound bacon
1 can sliced water chestnuts
1 bottle barbeque sauce (Open Pit, or your preferred brand)

Preheat oven to 350 degrees.
Cut bacon into thirds.
Wrap individual pieces around water chestnut slices. Fasten with toothpicks.
Bake in a baking dish (not a cookie sheet) for approximately 45 minutes, or until bacon is crisp.
Drain off grease and place on paper towels to absorb drippings.
Place back into clean baking dish and pour warmed barbeque sauce on top.

Dude's Cooking Flub

A lot of men can cook. Plenty more cannot. And then there are those who can't but think they can.

Linda Rice from my home state said she came home one night after a late meeting and was assaulted by a horrendous odor upon opening the front door.

"I followed the smell to the kitchen where I was expecting the worst," she said. "What I found was a kitchen gleaming and sparkling and smelling horrible."

Rice said she'd left the kitchen clean, but at this point it was immaculate.

She later discovered the origin of the smell from hell.

"It seems my husband had decided to fix hash browns and eggs and reached for the cooking oil and got Pine-Sol disinfectant cleaner instead."

Rice said she had no idea that when heated, pine oil spatters everywhere and changes odor.

On the bright side, Rice had a mother who washed her collards in the washing machine and painted her kitchen ceiling by standing on a chair with a brush in one hand and an umbrella in the other.

Burn, Baby, Burn . . . Kitchen Inferno

If there's one appliance I should never get near, it's the toaster oven. I've caught three on fire and ended up half-naked on my lawn with the fire department crew in my house trying to prevent the flames shooting from the toaster from igniting the walls and curtains.

I'm not alone. Other women (thank you, Lord) also succeed in cooking poorly enough to need firemen on the scene.

Meet Donna, one of my favorite mothers because she tells it like it is and is far from phony or full of baloney.

She caught her house on fire making *Kraft* Macaroni & Cheese.

"I was twenty at the time and renting a town house," she said. "In the midst of making the boxed mac and cheese, I realized I needed milk."

She cut the burner on low, figuring noodles would never pose a problem.

"I ran to the convenience store, which was a minute away," Donna said. "Yes, I know I should have turned the pot off." She was making good time until she ran into a friend at the store who needed a ride.

"It turned out to be farther than I realized, so I was hurrying. I didn't forget my mac and cheese, I just kept thinking that since it was on low it should be okay."

On the way back, she scurried into her town house to find it filled with smoke, alarm blaring.

"The bottom of the pot had completely burned away and there were little black bits that used to be macaroni."

Cooking While Drunk: Proof It Causes Trouble

Bobbie is Margie the Tooter's sister and equally as funny. She does a lot of entertaining, and in the late seventies was living the good life with her husband in Honolulu.

"I was very into the Time Life *Foods of the World* cookbooks," she said, "and I would theme my dinner parties around a certain country and do everything from soup to nuts using recipes from that country."

One evening, she chose a Russian-themed party, and was in charge of the food while her husband took over the booze department.

"He bought two bottles of Stolichnaya vodka to 'complement' my dinner. He then emptied two cartons of milk, filled them with water and froze the vodka in the ice, removing the milk cartons after they froze."

The night of the party, Bobbie was inundated with preparations and had no time for the vodka.

"We started with caviar on toast points and shots of vodka," she said. "Next came the Borsch and, of course, more shots. Next, a salad, Russian sweet bread and shots."

Then the Beef Stroganoff with Wide Noodles and shots.

Lastly, a wonderful fruit tart and more shots.

"By this time, I had joined in," Bobbie, a recovering boozer said. "I think I remember saying good-bye to our guests, but decided cleanup could wait 'til morning. Ugh! What a morning of dirty dishes and melted pools of water around the EMPTY vodka bottles.

"Later in the day, in bed with all the drapes closed, I got calls from our guests. They loved the cocktail party, but thought we were supposed to have dinner, too. No one remembered anything after the Borsch. Vodka will destroy the world."

Just ask Lindsay Lohan.

Bobbie's Beef Stroganoff

2 pounds sirloin beef, sliced thin
½ cup flour
5 Tbsp. butter
8 ounces sliced baby bella mushrooms
1½ cups sliced onions
¾ cup dry white wine
⅔ cup sour cream
1 package wide noodles

Melt butter in large cooking pot.
Brown meat, onions and mushrooms until softened.
Dredge with flour and pour in white wine.
Stir well until all flour has been absorbed in the sauce.
Simmer on very low heat until meat is very tender.
Stir in sour cream and immediately serve over wide noodles.

CHAPTER TWENTY-TWO

Eating Free, Buffet-a-Phobia, and Dubious Diets

I have a friend who's a nutritionist and deathly afraid of buffets. She calls her disorder Buffet-a-Phobia and says she is the opposite of her good friend Laurie, a caterer who calls herself a buffet-a-phile, someone who purely loves those all-you-can-eat joints.

Being somewhat mean (OK, a devilette in fake Prada) I invited Leah, the friend terrified of buffets, to my very favorite all-you-can-pack-in pig-out parlor, an Asian buffet with sushi and dozens of trays filled with deep-fried, stir-fried and sautéed items. I love to go there when absolutely famished from having skipped breakfast due to lack of time. As in the kids had bad hair, forgot to bathe, found no clothes worthy of their grandness and wouldn't eat their Cinnamon Life, making me late for work again.

While I'm of a fairly normal weight, having birdlike legs and a mother's stomach, I can eat as much as the 400-pounders who crack the chair legs and cause the proprietor to sweat his profit loss.

As I write this I can't breathe, having just inhaled four platters of sushi and other entrées at my favorite Asian buffet. I noticed (or was perhaps paranoid) the profit referee dinging the bell, running out with the muzzle, a big hatchet and calling for a TKO.

Total Knock Out.

"Hurry, hurry! Get this gulping, multitripper out of the restaurant!" I heard him saying in Chinese.

Yes, I realize I don't speak Chinese, but I can read body language and this is exactly what he was conveying.

As a result of not pulling back, I'm at my desk sitting like an overnursed puppy about to explode and release all stuffing.

Why can't I control my greed, portion size and snuffling sow's snout when placed before row upon row of high-calorie foods? I eat more at buffets than men and women who are seven times my weight. My tail wags like a dog's upon seeing a slab of tuna parts spread on steamed rice and seaweed.

If I could stop at the sushi, things wouldn't get out of control. But no. I have to Hoover all the other stuff, too: Sesame Chicken, Orange Chicken, Sweet-and-Sour Chicken, fried egg rolls, and wontons of every flavor and style.

It's gluttony and sinning worthy of altar call. Most of us do it (except the stick-bug starlets, who may do it, but follow pig-outs with purging).

There's a name for it, too. I recently read a story about this "binge eating" condition, citing the truth: everyone overeats every once in a while. Enough so they unbutton their waist-band, sprawl on the couch and wallow. A friend of mine said every Thanksgiving his family eats so much it's a tradition to lie on the living room floor and roll around moaning.

If this goes too far, then binge eating can be dangerous and is a topic addressed by many authors and excerpts, including Trisha Gura, author of *Lying in Weight: The Hidden Epidemic of Eating Disorders in Adult Women.*

Here is the test offered by Gura:

1. Q: Have you ever eaten a huge amount of food in a short period of time (say, more than 2,000 calories in two hours)?

A: Uh . . . yeah. Every time I go to a buffet. Everyone within two hundred yards takes cover and throws up a metal shield.

2. Q: Do you ever shovel food down, barely chewing, tasting or savoring what you are eating?

   A: Hmmm. Not really. I savor every bite, even if there are too many bites in a sitting.

3. Q: Do you sometimes, and perhaps often, eat alone in secret?

   A: No more so than Scarlett did before going to the picnic at Twelve Oaks.

4. Q: Do you ever find that your appetite or craving is so strong, you eat frozen or scalding-hot food?

   A: Sure do. Nothing beats raw cookie dough, until an hour passes and it "rises" in one's belly.

5. Q: Have you ever eaten food from your trash?

   A: No. I prefer other people's garbage.

The list of questions continued, but the news is good. While a serious health issue, binge eating is treatable. At least four million Americans have it. Professional help is recommended, so I'm not advocating running out and buying a log of raw Pillsbury dough or hitting the buffets until the owners run out screaming, "You gotta go home now. You costing me a fortune!"

I'm just saying it's a woman's right every now and then to sit at the pig trough guilt-free.

Men throw darts, guzzle spirits or bring home pelts.

Women? Carbs and credit cards do the trick.

If we overload and the scales become the enemy, I have a solution—three diets, each lasting three days, which is doable for even the hungriest of hoglets, me included.

I'm trying to get these diets approved, but I will say I've done all three and they work. I did not die. I lost about three pounds of water, thus reducing that awful feeling of bloating.

First up, irreverent but good Catholic girl DC Stanfa's sex diet, guaranteed to reduce weight by three pounds if done correctly.

The All-Sex, All-The-Time Diet

The All-Sex, All-The-Time-Diet—or the ASATD—not to be confused with an STD, which may also cause weight loss, but is not recommended because "feel the burn" isn't always a good thing.

Diet Preparation Checklist

1. Get a sitter for the kids.

2. Reserve a hotel room—with no view, but with well-insulated walls—and plan to order room service.

3. Get a virile (not viral) partner (free from STDs).

   (The main ingredient of this diet is not the food, it's the sexercise, which is much more fun than exercise. Plus, it burns calories, tones muscles and is a noncompetitive sport.)

4. Precool room to 60 degrees.

5. Order oysters, martinis and Viagra-stuffed olives.

6. Fill the bathtub with Jell-O, or Jell-O shots.

7. Sexercise, rinse, rest and repeat. (Baste generously, as necessary.)

Your results will vary, depending on your sexertion. An average of 120 calories per hour, times, let's say, ten hours a day, times three days, should burn a total of 3,600 calories. And afterward you will be able to crack coconuts with your thighs.*

**Level of sexual exertion. Mild sexertion burns 108 calories per hour,* *while moderate sexertion consumes 120. However, engaging in a 15- to 20-minute wrestling match throws down 180. Side effects include rug burns, an addiction to Spandex and use of words like "pulverize."*

Susan Reinhardt's Three-Day, Three-Pound-Loss, Pain-in-the Ass Diet
(Hey, but it works.)

If you're like me, you hate feeling bloated. The older you get the more you bloat, the more you bloat the WORSE you feel, so avoid the bloat at every meal. Here's how:

1. For breakfast the next three days, enjoy a tall eight-ounce glass of water followed by six to ten raw, unsalted almonds. Green tea is better for weight loss than coffee, which stimulates the appetite. Personally, I'd rather have the coffee and deal with the stimulation of hunger.

2. One hour later eat some of that Quaker Oats "Weight Control" high-protein oatmeal served in single packets.

3. Buy a whole bunch of low-fat yogurts—the kind with about 100 calories. Three times a day, you can have one or two of them. Never go over four or six.

4. For protein, buy those cute little cans of tuna or salmon in water and slather with some yummy Duke's mayo. You don't even have to get the low-fat kind 'cause they're yucky and the fat in the mayo will help curb hunger. Use about a hefty teaspoon and mix. Add lemon and celery and onion if you like. You can eat this twice a day.

5. Eat fruit only if you've had nothing in your stomach for at least an hour or two. Eat two to three fruits a day.

6. Enjoy one or two big salads a day. This means lettuce, raw veggies and one teaspoon of yummy regular dress-

ing. No use making yourself sick and deprived by trying to choke down that nasty diet dressing.

If you want to burn more calories than you can on the Sex Diet, due to lack of interest or partner, then let me suggest hot yoga for 1.5 hours. Don't wuss out and take one of those stretch-and-pose yoga classes. What we're talking about here is a hard-core, heart-pumping, sweat-pouring class such as Kundalini. For more on this go to *www.kundaliniyoga.org.*

Every time I do the class (this is the one with Andie MacDowell in it), I wake up the next day two pounds lighter.

If you don't have access to this mother of all yoga classes, then walk for forty-five minutes or three miles.

Remember, my diet is all about threes. Three days, three pounds.

Use this daily, with the meal items in any order, and watch the bloat retreat.

The Hip L.A. Lawyer Diet

My friend Pauline is an ultracool lawyer (not an oxymoron in this case), from Los Angeles, who used to run marathons, has done aerobics with movie stars and worked out with world-known trainers.

She can drop pounds quicker than Whitney on a crack pipe. She learned how to cook—a few dishes—shortly after a mishap with macaroni and cheese, but her main expertise is in whittling flab.

Here's her plan:

Breakfast: 1½ packs oatmeal* with 2 egg whites stirred in (This can include 3 tablespoons of sugar-free syrup, flavor of your choice.)

*Blueberry and gingerbread are excellent, a lean Pauline reports.

Morning snack: 1 low-fat yogurt

Lunch: Salad or soup, chicken or tuna with diet salad dressing

Afternoon snack: 1 cup cottage cheese.

Dinner: Turkey or (chicken breast) and vegetables

Snack: Diet pudding cup or a Fudgesicle

This woman weighs 110 pounds with bricks in her jeans. I'm trying to fatten her up.

If following a restricted food plan is not your bag, there's always TrimTalk, a diet support group that utilizes the telephone to talk people into thin and healthy living.

I kid you not. This hotline involves weight consulting by phone and includes chat rooms, counselors, and most importantly, "no embarrassing public weigh-ins."

Let's give space to the issue of public weigh-ins.

Sugahs, it's not a rule. I've tried to tell friends and loved ones that it is their legal right to flat-out refuse to step on a set of scales. The first time I utilized my right to Just Say No was a few years ago during a routine physical.

The nurse had pumped furiously to find a blood pressure, twice failing, then decided I was alive after all, and ordered me to hop up on her scales. We all know doctor's office scales are cruelty devices and that our home units always give us the weight we seek.

If I wake up bloated and my little $10 floor model flashes a number I simply can't live with, then I tweak it backward until the digits make for a joyful day.

I know it's not accurate, but one has to do certain things in order not to jump off a parkway overlook. Sadly, one can't do this at the doctor's office; they don't cotton to a patient recalibrating their high-end scales.

So here's what you do:

The nurse smiles and says, "Mrs. So-and-So, I do believe your blood pressure has decided to stay in bed for the day. Let's see if we can't get a weight on you."

This is when you say. . . .

"I'd rather not, if it's all the same to you, thank you very much."

She will look at you as if you are an errant child in need of a time-out, but then she remembers the Patient's Bill of Rights, which I think has a section called, "Don't force a woman to weigh," but I'm not certain.

Remember, you don't have to weigh unless your condition is serious or you are pregnant.

Now, for that TrimTalk business. I feel certain it's kind of like phone sex but involves food instead. Like those 1-900 numbers where the women carry on like a fleet of harlots, TrimTalk probably has professionals gently coaxing a person out of sinking her molars into a six-pack of Little Debbie Swiss Cake Rolls.

I feel confident they tell one to visualize his or herself at the ocean with gentle waves rolling in. Every self-help group I have ever come across uses that old ocean-wave trick. Why don't they realize it's outdated and doesn't work?

Tell us instead to visualize Matthew McConaughey in a tight tee and some Levi's 501. Tell us if we refuse a bag of Nestlé Semi-Sweet Morsels, we'll win his love and he'll invite Patrick Dempsey from *Grey's Anatomy* over for a bonus.

Since that isn't going to happen, I decided to save my money and use my own version of TrimTalk, called "Phone A Friend."

I call Andi Kdan, a nurse who also hates to bloat, every other night and tell her I'm swelling, Gerding and in need of a diuretic.

She then tells me she can't button her pants, though I know she very well can, and that she just made a huge plate of nachos and will polish them off before going to bed.

For some reason, this makes me feel so much better as I climb under the covers, Pecan Sandies dusting my comforter.

P.S. Since writing this book, I've learned to cook a few more meals and am planning to take a cooking class or two.

I've also gained twenty pounds from take-out and PMS and the dreaded . . . bloat!

To all the kitchen virgins in this world, there is hope. To all the kitchen hos—watch out. With a few lessons and the right recipes, who knows what the future will hold?

P.P.S. I doubt I will ever go to that cooking class. Just to be honest.

Recipe Index